PRAISE FOR *CRISIS COMMUNICATION STRATEGIES*, SECOND EDITION

'If you are a communicator trying to navigate a more unpredictable world, this book is a timely and valuable guide. Drawing on a range of case studies, Amanda Coleman clearly sets out the plans, processes and procedures you need to put in place to be prepared when a crisis strikes. But more importantly, she recognises the fundamental importance of people – from CEOs to customers, terrorism victims and communicators themselves – to effective crisis communication and recovery.'

Oana Lungescu, NATO spokesperson

'This is a book that does something special and really different in crisis communications. It is definitive on the immense organizational challenges but also holds those affected by the crisis to the heart of the approach. A must read.'

Professor Lucy Easthope, disaster recovery specialist and author

'There is a major focus on preparing to issue rapid and accurate communications when a crisis happens. But in this second edition of her acclaimed handbook, the widely admired Amanda Coleman goes beyond the early hours to take us through every stage of a crisis, including recovery. Her practical approach is forged through real-life experience. This new edition is required reading for public relations professionals and leaders who wish to understand the role of communications in a crisis. It should be in every company library.'

Donald Steel, global crisis communications practitioner and Vice-President, Crisis Communications, at Kenyon International Emergency Services

'In a crisis you need people, plans and professionalism to keep a level head. *Crisis Communication Strategies* is a step-by-step, expert guide to the critical early legwork, staying afloat in the eye of the storm and managing the transition to recovery. Jam-packed with learnings from real-life crisis case studies, Amanda Coleman has put her years of experience into creating a clear framework for people to follow. If you're a CEO or any director focused on risk and resilience, this book is your critical friend. Grab a copy now.'
Sarah Waddington CBE, Director, Wadds Inc

'Making a great resource even better, Amanda Coleman's second edition of her outstanding book adds new material on the critical issues facing organizations today. She provides step-by-step guidance, checklists and tips for handling crisis communication successfully. This book should be on every leader and communication professional's desk as an invaluable reference for handling one of the most important aspects of any crisis – how the organization explains it to the public and key stakeholders. I wish I had this book when I first moved into the crisis communication field.'
Bob Jensen, Senior Managing Director, Strat3 LLC

'The second edition of *Crisis Communication Strategies* proves again that Amanda Coleman is one of the best practitioners out there. It is well written, easy to read and covers a variety of topics and stakeholders that are important for crisis communication to succeed in 2023. What I value the most is that Coleman includes so much practical advice that will be useful for communicators around the world. I can highly recommend this book to anyone interested in the field of crisis communication.'
Kjell Braatas, communications adviser and author

Crisis Communication Strategies

Prepare, respond and recover effectively in unpredictable and urgent situations

SECOND EDITION

Amanda Coleman

KoganPage

First published in Great Britain and the United States in 2020 by Kogan Page Limited
Second edition published in 2023

2nd Floor, 45 Gee Street	8 W 38th Street, Suite 902	4737/23 Ansari Road
London	New York, NY 10018	Daryaganj
EC1V 3RS	USA	New Delhi 110002
United Kingdom		India
www.koganpage.com		

Kogan Page books are printed on paper from sustainable forests.

© Amanda Coleman, 2020, 2023

ISBNs
Hardback   978 1 3986 0944 0
Paperback   978 1 3986 0941 9
Ebook   978 1 3986 0942 6

British Library Cataloguing-in-Publication Data
A CIP record for this book is available from the British Library.

Library of Congress Cataloging-in-Publication Data
Names: Coleman, Amanda, author.
Title: Crisis communication strategies : prepare, respond and recover effectively in unpredictable and urgent situations / Amanda Coleman.
Description: Second Edition. | New York, NY : Kogan Page Inc, 2023. | Revised edition of the author's Crisis communication strategies, 2020. | Includes bibliographical references and index.
Identifiers: LCCN 2022055450 (print) | LCCN 2022055451 (ebook) | ISBN 9781398609419 (paperback) | ISBN 9781398609440 (hardback) | ISBN 9781398609426 (ebook)
Subjects: LCSH: Communication in crisis management. | Crisis management.
Classification: LCC HD49.3 .C65 2023 (print) | LCC HD49.3 (ebook) | DDC 658.4/5–dc23/eng/20221121
LC record available at https://lccn.loc.gov/2022055450
LC ebook record available at https://lccn.loc.gov/2022055451

Typeset by Hong Kong FIVE Workshop
Print production managed by Jellyfish
Printed and bound by CPI Group (UK) Ltd, Croydon CR0 4YY

This book is dedicated to those who have provided me with endless amounts of support, who have believed in me and have encouraged me throughout the years. It is particularly dedicated to my Dad and my late Mum (Philip and Prue) who have given me determination and helped me reach for the stars. Also to my furry companions Digger and particularly Edward, who was my soulmate for 19 years and sadly died just as this edition was being finalized.

CONTENTS

LIST OF FIGURES AND TABLES

ABOUT THE AUTHOR

Amanda Coleman is a PR and communication professional with extensive experience of managing communication when dealing with crises. She is the director of her own crisis communication consultancy and works with a wide variety of clients providing both training and support to deal with crises. Amanda is a Fellow of both the Chartered Institute of Public Relations and the Public Relations and Communications Association, as well as being a Chartered PR Practitioner. Amanda is the author of *Everyday Communication Strategies*, also published by Kogan Page. She writes a blog under the name Amandacomms Blog (amandacomms1.wordpress.com).

PREFACE

After many years dealing with crises and developing effective communication strategies to deal with whatever had occurred I wanted to find a way to share my experience and help other communicators. At times it seemed that I was dealing with a new crisis on a daily basis and they became the norm. But for many PR and communication professionals a crisis may happen just once in their career and they will be thrown into a high-stakes and high-pressure environment. I hope this book will encourage people to think about crises, and to develop plans and prepare for when it happens. In short it is about investing some time to be able to deal with the darkest day a business is likely to face.

From all my experience it became clear that there were some aspects of the crisis communication in both planning and response that were not being considered. In short it boils down to one word – and that is people. We have spent time, possibly, in establishing plans, processes or procedures but I would be fairly sure that none of them have taken adequate account of the impact on people. This is people both within the organization and, importantly, those who are affected by the crisis. Those are the aspects that I wanted to focus on, and to encourage others to refresh their approach to crisis communication.

This new edition includes consideration of how behavioural change communication can support a crisis response, how to ensure a focus on diversity and inclusion is maintained even when under pressure, and how to remain resilient when dealing with a long-running crisis. Since the first edition in 2020 the Covid-19 pandemic, aftermath, war in Europe and extreme weather have all expanded our knowledge and experience of facing crises and developing appropriate communication. I have reflected this in the updates within this edition.

The book covers the whole span of the crisis from the time before it happens, during the incident and the aftermath, including the move to recovery. It aims to guide you through each phase, providing details of what to consider, what should be done and tips on improving your response. Alongside this there are a number of case studies detailing where organizations have responded to a crisis, showing where things worked well and where they could have been improved.

Anyone dealing with communication planning and strategy development will benefit from the advice within this book, but equally, if you are a senior manager or CEO who will have to respond to a crisis, this book can provide assistance. Having the right knowledge and understanding is the first step to developing an effective crisis communication strategy. If you are going to be ready to respond then you need to invest time now.

ACKNOWLEDGEMENTS

In developing this book I have to thank all those who have supported me in good times and bad, as well as the Chartered Institute of Public Relations and the Public Relations and Communications Association. Special thanks to Christine Townsend for her assistance. I am grateful to the team at Kogan Page for their continued support, as well as the clients, organizations and businesses that working with has assisted in the development of the book. A special thank you to those on social media who provided suggestions for what to include in this updated second edition.

1

Are you ready for a crisis? Creating and testing a crisis communication plan

Every communication professional knows there will come a day when they must face a crisis. The test is how they deal with it and if the response is both efficient and effective. It is the moment in time that can make or break careers. If it is done well it will be the making of the individual or team, providing them with a wealth of experience and knowledge that will benefit future work. When things go wrong with the communication response it can impact negatively on people, share prices and ultimately can decimate a brand. Being ready for a crisis is essential for every organization, company or brand. Dealing with a crisis requires a different approach and a specific set of skills when compared to everyday communication. Crisis communication has a level of intensity and risk involved that means the communicator needs to be operating at the peak of their performance. They must be ready to spring into action, to rally the troops to deliver the response, to balance the demands and to have the resilience to steer the organization through the crisis and out to recovery. Preparation is the foundation to the success of a response and must have taken place. The speed of communication required in the eye of the storm of a crisis increases the possibility of a critical element, of the issue or the response, being missed. There are many facets of the communication that need to be operating at the same time and spinning the plates is a test for even the most seasoned crisis communicator.

Comments, views and criticism will be coming from many places, which can quickly put a company in a defensive position. Being defensive will be identified by onlookers and the public, who see this as a negative approach. The nature of some crises can make them feel incredibly personal both to the management and the workers in the business. For an in-house communicator or those working closely with a brand this can be strongly felt, and those emotions, alongside the pressure on the resilience of those involved, can lead to unexpected plans for action rooted in emotion rather than fact. It requires an ability to be acutely aware of the emotions around the crisis but to be able to step away from it to provide an intelligent and strategic response. Developing this ability to step into and out of the crisis will be discussed in more detail in the coming chapters.

Every element of the response to the incident will be scrutinized and analysed both during and after the crisis. This includes the operational response and the success of communication, which is always a key area to review. With crises that are handled by emergency services the debriefs are often critical of elements of communication, from a slow response through to a failure to connect and engage with those who are affected. From the statements or actions of the CEO through to the comments made by customer services and frontline staff, all will be under the microscope instantly. The Gjørv report into the response to the 2011 Oslo bombing and Utøya massacre in Norway was delivered to the prime minister just over a year later and considered in detail the police response and communication that took place with the public (see the case study on page 25). Similarly the extreme weather conditions and Storm Arwen in 2022 led to scrutiny and reviews of the response, which included assessing the communication that was undertaken (see the case study on page 27).

Controlling the narrative

Public response, feedback and the commentary from those caught up in the incident can quickly become the narrative of the incident or issue. Narrative is the story of the events, and all those connected will have their approach and viewpoint on the crisis. Within a very short period one version of events will become the accepted statement of the situation and this can last for some time even through to an investigation or public inquiry. A company or organization must work to ensure its commentary on the situation is the one that becomes the dominant narrative and the trusted information about what has occurred. If this is achieved then it is on its way to building trust and confidence through showing understanding, taking action and demonstrating learning. All this is more likely to be achieved if work to define the response to a crisis has been undertaken in the quiet moments when the business can take care and time to consider how the response will be delivered. Given the pressure and speed of a crisis, there is no chance to develop a crisis communication plan from scratch when an issue or incident is unravelling on social media and on rolling news channels. Having a plan, systems and procedures in place will save precious time and put the business into a proactive position quickly. It is not just about having a plan but about testing whether it is likely to work as a response. Beyond that, the work must not just be completed but it must also be embedded into the business as a key cog in the organization's response. The business can then act swiftly when a crisis happens.

Communication thrives on creativity. This will be restricted when a crisis occurs as the freedom that leads to creativity must be replaced with a systematic approach to the sharing of information. In the initial stages of a crisis a cool head is needed and being able to turn to a clear plan will build some resilience for the communicators involved. There will be time enough to develop a creative approach to the problem at hand once you have faced what is emerging and put things in place after the crisis breaks. Systems and procedures are what will help to calm the pressure on communicating in the initial stages of a crisis. Despite the many benefits that come from having a plan ready to launch at a moment's notice, organizations are still reluctant to put enough time and effort into the development of a clear crisis response system with a plan and procedure.

The crisis communication strategy and approach are only as good as the scenario planning and testing of the processes. This must be more than a theoretical development of something that will sit on a shelf or languish somewhere in the company's databases. More about the implementation and embedding of the plan within the business later in this chapter.

TOP TIP

Take some time to consider what plans you have in place to deal with a crisis or emergency the business may face. Does it stand alone? Is it part of an organizational response plan? Have you considered the main risks the business may face?

It is essential to understand what you may already have in place to help in the response to a crisis. If there are plans in place, then review them considering the guidance and advice you will find in the pages of this book. Consider if the plan you have puts communication as a key part of the overall response. The activity of the communication team must align to the response of the organization, and, as will be explained later in this book, it can help to drive the organization's response.

Strategy or plan?

There is often confusion about what comprises a communication strategy and what is a plan. It is important to be clear about which of these you are developing before you set out to write or update a crisis document. A crisis communication strategy sets out the high-level approach to be taken when dealing with any issue or incident. It will consider the management of channels, including media and social media, and any policies that need to be in place or linked to the strategy.

In contrast, a crisis communication plan is a tactical document that looks at the specific situation and considers the actions that need to be taken at key points as the crisis emerges, develops and then ends. This will be a roadmap for managing communication when a situation occurs. The documents must be connected and work together to ensure an effective crisis communication response. However, it is important to understand the distinction between the two so that both elements are developed in a crisis response.

The most important starting point is to have a clear crisis communication strategy that can be understood by the communication professional and everyone else working in or supporting the business' crisis response. It will be the framework for responding to any crisis, whether it is reputational or operational. An operational crisis is something that has happened in the environment around us. Something that emerges due to world events or due to an operational issue within the business. Reputational crises are rooted in perceptions and commentary. They do not require anything physical to have happened as they can be due to something that has been said either online or in the media. We will explore this further in the following chapter.

For any crisis communication strategy, simplicity is key, both for ensuring that anyone can pick the document up and understand what the approach will be and what their role is, and for the ability to use it for every crisis that may occur. Details and step-by-step guides to responding to a crisis should be included in a plan. But it must avoid being restrictive and should allow development and new approaches to the situation to be considered in the response. Plans should follow themes or risk areas so that they are not covering just one set of circumstances alone as invariably this will not be the situation that emerges when a crisis hits. For example, planning for a cyberattack that steals personal data when what happens is a ransomware attack that blocks systems and demands money. Both are cyber crises but require slightly different tactical approaches.

Every crisis is unique and has its own very distinct set of circumstances. If you have a pre-prepared response that lacks flexibility then your communication will miss the target and fail to respond to what is emerging. Relying on a plan without thinking and considering exactly what you are faced with will lead to a poor response. It is more beneficial to have a broader, more strategic document as a crisis communication plan; a document that considers approach, provides prompts, outlines clear roles and includes checklists that can support the response to any set of circumstances. It is a foundation to assist in dealing with any crisis. This works closely with a crisis communication strategy outlining the organization's approach to all issues, incidents and emergencies.

The crisis communication strategy

The key sections of a crisis communication strategy are:

- purpose of the strategy
- approach
- communication priorities
- structure of the response, phases of a crisis – roles and responsibilities
- scenarios, narratives and key messages
- priority channels
- stakeholder engagement
- resourcing
- review and evaluation

Other elements may be required for individual businesses and organizations, such as brand management or shareholder communication.

Being ready for a crisis goes beyond having a plan on paper or hidden in a database – it is essential to consider how the strategy and approach is shared, communicated, tested and developed further. However, having a strategy and plan in place is a fundamental first step to being prepared to manage a crisis. Let's look now at each stage of the strategy and what it should cover.

Purpose of the strategy

In this section, outline the responsibilities that the business or organization has in responding to a crisis. For example, if you have responsibilities under legislation then make it clear what these are and what they may mean for your communication response. The legislative process may lead to some restrictions on what you can do, and these must be understood before developing a response. Outline the details of when and how the approach will be used and how it will fit with any organizational crisis response. The preference is always to have a communication strategy that will be a section or chapter of any business' crisis or emergency response manual. However, if this doesn't exist and it must sit alone then ensure there are links to any other corporate strategies.

FIGURE 1.1   Relationship between crisis communication plan and the organizational response plans

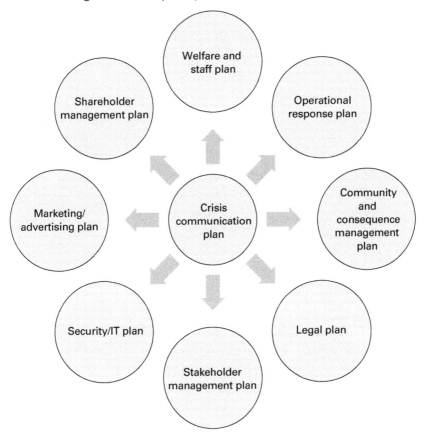

Approach

The organization will have its own vision, mission and philosophy and this should influence the approach to be taken to communicating in a crisis. Consider what you want people to say about the business and what it is known to stand for, such as amazing customer service or taking an ethical approach to business, and ensure this is reflected in the approach you plan to take when dealing with a crisis. Handled effectively, crisis communication can enhance and build the organization's reputation and strengthen the vision, mission or philosophy among the workforce and the public.

Communication priorities

This is the section where you can outline the priority actions for the communication response through the stages of a crisis, from recognizing the issue or incident and the first phases of the crisis, developing the response, re-establishing the status quo and finally the move to recovery. Consider within this whether the organization will be leading the response or whether you are working alongside other organizations or agencies that may be taking the lead. Provide details of the activities that you will undertake during the initial phase of the crisis, which may include alerting the CEO, implementing the response structure and calling in additional resources. If there is a necessity to contact key stakeholders before providing any response then make this clear in the priorities.

RESPONSE CHECKLIST

Initial response

- Grab bag – have a bag that is filled with essentials that the first communicator dealing with the incident will need. This could include a USB stick loaded with the plan and any prepared short holding statements (holding statements are developed to buy the business some time before making a more detailed response), details of additional resources and contact information, and other relevant items such as building access information, emergency mobile phone or other technology that will assist. (It is common that technology may be found lacking in the initial stages of an emergency so it is important to have access to back-up systems.) This could also be supported by a virtual grab bag, which is a folder containing all relevant information. But avoid leaving all documents online, as if there is a power outage it will mean key information cannot be accessed.

- Contact the operational lead to gather enough information that is accurate at that moment in time and can be used to support the development of the first statements. Remember never to assume or expand on information unless you are sure at that moment it is accurate.

- If another organization or agency is taking the lead on the communication and operational response contact it to be clear what can be stated publicly.

- Provide an initial statement as swiftly as possible. It may state nothing more than that you are aware of the issue, incident or situation and that you are dealing with it or assessing the situation and will provide more detail as it becomes available, or that you are working with another lead agency. This ensures that people can see you are aware something is happening and are acting.

- Start a rolling log of what information has been provided, who authorized it and what communication decisions have been made. This can become invaluable as time passes as it will provide clarity about what has been said, when it was said, who said it and who it was provided to, such as to specific media outlets or placed on social media.

- Contact the relevant people or agencies who will provide additional resources as the situation develops. An early alert will mean the additional resources arrive more swiftly.

Response in first 24 hours

- Use the crisis communication plan that has been developed to create a bespoke plan that will focus on the detail of the scenario you are faced with.

- Identify the key spokesperson for the company/organization and ensure they are briefed on the situation and what has currently been provided via media/social media, and are ready to appear publicly to provide updates.

- Ensure media and social media are being monitored and relevant data is being gathered, including commentary that may need to be corrected as well as understanding the sentiment of the comments.

- Establish the structure of the communication response and ensure key roles are being undertaken; this includes internal messaging and stakeholder engagement, and remember to consider the welfare of those involved, including any communication staff.
- Provide a regular time for updates to be given to the media, social media or other audiences, even if this is just to restate what information is known and accurate.

Developing activity

- Consider whether greater access can be provided to the media, bloggers or others to show the care and attention being given to dealing with the issue.
- Work with operational staff to identify those affected and manage communication to them either directly or indirectly depending on the scale of the issue.
- Ensure that by this stage you have the relevant stakeholder engagement plan in place and that you are sharing statements and encouraging others to assist in a shared narrative about the issue or incident.
- Ensure you have enough resources for the next week to four weeks, including to cover activities at weekends and overnight. Are your on-call arrangements sufficiently robust during the response phase?
- Be clear when and how updates will be provided and utilize the same spokesperson wherever possible to ensure continuity.
- Consider how to be creative in the communication to assist in rebuilding confidence in the organization or brand.

Re-establishing status quo

- Identify when you can resume 'normal' business. This will require careful discussion with the operational lead dealing with the issue, and the CEO. Once you have a clear time frame you can start to scale back the resources being used for communication activity.
- Be clear with people who have been following updates on the incident about when and how they will receive further information once the crisis is over.

- Use creative communication to update the shared narrative and always provide an explanation of why the move towards recovery is now taking place.

- Keep any public telephone or digital helplines running if they are receiving relevant calls. As the calls subside replace them with existing communication methods and ensure this is clearly understood.

- Review the communication activity and evaluation that has taken place to identify further work that may be required to rebuild trust and confidence.

Road to recovery

A later chapter in the book will deal with the difficult decision of when to start to move the operational activity and communication activity into the recovery phase (see Chapter 8).

Structure of the response: Including roles and responsibilities

As mentioned, taking a systematic approach to crisis communication can provide a greater opportunity for a successful response. Whether you are working in-house, for an agency or as a consultant you can still clearly outline the structure that will be in place to provide the required response. Consider how you will be able to get decisions from within the business and how much flexibility there is for communication to be developed and implemented without a sign-off process. Governance is an essential part of a communication strategy as it establishes delegated authority, and the way actions and statements are agreed. A clear decision-making process needs to be outlined along with any communication sign-off protocols. The best position is to have ensured the leadership of the organization have confidence in the communication team and the preparation work that has been undertaken to allow some flexibility and autonomy in the initial stages.

PHASES OF A CRISIS

While much of our focus is on the starting point of a crisis and ensuring that it is identified, a crisis has many phases and each needs careful consideration when defining the approach to take. There are five broadly defined phases of a crisis and the elements that comprise each of them will also require a change, refinement or development of the communication approach and activity that is being undertaken.

1 Identification

2 Initial actions

3 Eye of the storm

4 Pre-recovery

5 Recovery

The operational response will be different within each of these phases. For example, in the identification phase the key will be about ensuring key people are briefed and aware of what has happened, and that the crisis response plan has been implemented. When in the eye of the storm it is essential that the focus is on tactical actions being taken to minimize the impact of the crisis and ensure things are brought under control. Each of these phases also requires crisis communication to be handled slightly differently to ensure the focus is on the key and relevant issues, and the potential changes within people's attitudes to what has occurred.

1 Identification
This is the point at which the crisis has been recognized and identified and has been highlighted within the organization. Communication needs to be involved from the earliest possible point so that an initial comment can be made and plans can start to be developed.

2 Initial actions
Dealing with the first moments of a crisis, and particularly the first 24 hours, will set the scene for how things may develop. It is the point where plans and strategies need to be considered, reviewed and developed as required. It is also a point where resourcing for the crisis response needs to be considered and additional support sourced if needed. This is the point where the

crisis communication plan is agreed and in place, immediate actions have been completed and the structures, resourcing and narrative are agreed.

3 Eye of the storm

After the initial urgent actions have been carried out and work is underway, the next phase is moving towards addressing the problem. This phase can last for a few days or for years and the long-term crises require additional considerations, which we will cover in Chapter 8. The eye of the Covid-19 pandemic storm lasted for more than a year in many parts of the world. It is this stage when activities and a plan need to be in place. The plans should centre around engagement following the broadcast approach of the initial stages, and ensuring the approach is inclusive and reaches all communities is essential. It is also during this phase that plans must be developed using consultation, and actions evaluated.

4 Pre-recovery

Once the whirlwind centre of the crisis has happened there is a stage where the situation is being brought under control and its impact is reducing. But the crisis is still underway, so it is not the recovery phase. This is a time to start to consider the recovery phase but recognize that activities are still managing the crisis. It is also important to be aware that at any point something may happen to move you back towards the eye of the storm. There is a delicate balancing act to be carried out between continuing to deliver the crisis communication plan, and creating and implementing the recovery communication plan. It requires the communicator to be very aware of developments, possible future scenarios and the state of the operational response.

5 Recovery

This is the point at which the crisis is under control and has ended. It is a time when the organization can review what has happened, rebuild from what was happening before the crisis, consider the required resourcing and move to re-establish the reputation of the business or organization. For the communicator it means moving from a crisis communication plan to a recovery communication plan (see Chapter 8).

Each phase of the crisis will take as long as it needs to and cannot be rushed. The identification needs to be undertaken swiftly to put steps in place that can begin to manage what has happened. But in some cases identifying the crisis can take longer to achieve. If the business or organization attempts to move quickly then it can potentially damage the confidence people have in the response. Always be clear at what point in the crisis you are so that appropriate communication can be undertaken.

ESTABLISHING ROLE PROFILES

Establish clear role profiles that identify the actions and span of control of each of the team members involved in the response. The profiles can be used for any non-communicators that are brought in to support the communication response, as well as agency or free-lance staff who are recruited to assist. If you are delivering the response alone (and this is not a recommended position to be in) then you can use the profiles to ensure you are developing a response that covers all the critical areas of communication activity. Among the roles to consider having in place is communication leader, usually the most senior communication professional working on the crisis and will report to the organization's spokesperson, who will provide the face of the response. They will operate at 'Gold' level, which will be outlined in Chapter 3. In many cases the spokesperson will be the CEO but it will be dependent on the nature of the issue or incident as it may be more appropriate for another senior executive to be the face of the response. The communication leader is a professional who will set the strategy and keep it under review as the situation develops. Depending on the nature of the incident and the size of the crisis they may be able to manage the implementation of the strategy or may have a deputy to assist in making the strategy live. Other roles to consider having in place are internal communication lead, partnership lead, affected people lead, digital communication lead, staff wellbeing lead (this may be part of the internal communication lead role but if the impact on resilience and wellbeing of the workforce is significant then a separate role is recommended) and a media/social media monitoring lead. This is not an exhaustive list and in different business sectors it may be that additional roles are required. The key to establishing which roles are relevant is to understand who the key stakeholders or groups are that you will need to connect with during a crisis. Map out who they are and understand what impact there will be if there is a failure to adequately connect, brief, inform and listen to them during a crisis. This should then provide you with a clear picture of the roles that are required to manage communication activity.

Scenarios and key messages

As mentioned earlier, having very fixed messages that will be used for every crisis regardless of the specific details of the event being managed is not recommended. The first thing to do when considering what messages may be appropriate to have in place is to have detailed the most likely scenarios that the business will face. Scenarios may include a cyberattack, product or service failure, or a disgruntled ex-employee going public with criticism of the business – and there will be many others that you can consider, linked to the nature of the business. If you are not sure where to start, then consider reviewing the organization's risk management plan or risk register as this will detail possible threats. Once you have the scenarios then you can develop some initial key messages based on the likely issues. Focus on key points such as providing helpline numbers, detailing that you are aware of the issue and are responding to it, and any key information you can provide that will demonstrate a swift response and that the issue is being taken seriously. Wherever possible provide ways that the public can assist in the response, such as providing information, keeping away from the area, returning any damaged goods. All this will provide you with a starting point when a crisis emerges, which allows a swift response and gives some space to consider the detailed responses that need to be developed. The key messages are there as a guide and need to be adapted to the issue or incident that occurs.

Priority channels

Managing a crisis requires using all acquired knowledge from previous work. The strategies that already exist will provide understanding of where the business' priority audiences get their information and where they will turn to for updates in the moment a crisis emerges. The number of social media sites and digital platforms that exist is overwhelming and trying to service all of them will be an uphill struggle. Instead of spreading things thinly across all digital platforms, focus on where the key audiences are and identify those channels that you will prioritize within the plan. For example, if you have a strong presence on Facebook or LinkedIn then identify those as priority channels within your communication response. However, do not neglect other more traditional channels of communication such as local media, face-to-face communication, helpdesks and frontline workers. The key is to put the effort of the communication response where it will have the biggest impact and that requires understanding audiences and having detailed insight about customers.

Stakeholder engagement

We have already touched on this when we considered scenarios and how they can support the development of key messages. Conducting a stakeholder mapping exercise is important for all aspects of communication activity. It will ensure the business understands who its key audiences and influencers are, which becomes critical during a crisis. Communicating to those groups, whether they are shareholders, investors, regulators or partner agencies is essential throughout the crisis. It can build trust and confidence in the business and demonstrate that it has the situation under control, and in turn that will develop strong future relationships. Be clear who is important to connect with during a crisis; as we will see, ensuring they know the plan in detail will become an important part of the preparation for dealing with any crisis.

Resourcing

The intensity of a crisis is like nothing a communicator will have experienced before. With rolling news channels and social media sites it is a round-the-clock responsibility, and it takes a significant number of people to be able to deliver the plan effectively. In developing the roles and responsibilities section you will gain a greater understanding of the number of people required to manage the response. This is important so that you can ensure there is access to the resources, and this can be achieved within a short time frame. First understand what resources you need, and then identify where they will come from. The plans and mechanisms need to be in place to draw in additional people if required either from across the business or from external agencies. Successfully emerging from a crisis will take time, effort and care, which all requires enough resources to be in place. Ensure you continue to consider the resources that are required through to completion of the recovery phase. Once you have identified where resources will come from, ensure that the individuals or teams understand what role they will play. This will be covered in more detail later in this chapter when we consider how the plan should be promoted within the business and how to ensure a level of preparedness exists.

RESOURCES MAY BE DRAWN FROM:

- communication staff
- others with communication knowledge or experience
- individuals who may have been on secondment to the communication team
- mutual aid (identify staff within partner agencies or businesses who may be brought in to assist)
- agency staff
- freelancers or retained external contracted staff

Review and evaluation

Traditional methods of evaluation will not benefit the crisis communication in the initial stages of the response. However, building in the ability to review the impact of the activity is essential. Ensure that your plan identifies how and when the communication work will be reviewed and assessed. There may be key trigger points that prompt a move to review or evaluate the activity, such as when a key operational activity is carried out. The information gathered will inform the development of the plan by clarifying what has worked and what gaps still exist. Both review and evaluation are very different to the media monitoring that is required throughout a crisis. Media monitoring is about understanding what is being said on social media and in the traditional media so that inaccuracies can be corrected, and the messaging and activity can be refined. Evaluating the crisis communication plan is about a longer-term understanding of the organization's reputation and trust and confidence in the business. This should happen at key points, likely to be part-way through the operational response, at the end of the crisis phase as the business is moving into recovery, and then as the recovery phase is ending. This is when the existing methods of evaluating communication activity can be brought to the fore. Check out the AMEC Integrated Evaluation Framework[1] to provide some guidance and clarity on areas of measurement that can be undertaken. It is important for the evaluation to consider outputs, outcomes and outtakes for all the work as well as the organizational impact of the activities undertaken. Reviewing and evaluating will support the prioritization of activities and ensure that effort is being put where it is needed the most.

Earlier we discussed having the right technology at your fingertips the minute a crisis emerges. A laptop and smartphone are essentials to have with you or easily accessible so you can utilize them instantly. Statements and replies need to be posted on the organization's website and social media so ensure there is access to any platforms and systems. This means having the right passwords that will allow quick access. If the organization has controls that prevent access to social media on business computers, then consider having a non-networked computer that can be used. Technology can assist in the creative development of communication as the crisis continues and this will be considered in a later chapter.

Sharing the crisis communication plan

Once you have invested time in developing a crisis communication plan you are part of the way to having established readiness for any emerging issue or incident that may occur. The next step is to ensure that the details of the plan are shared with the business. Why is this important? It will ensure that the plan is clearly understood by all those who are likely to be involved in any crisis response, which includes the CEO, key department heads, customer services staff and anyone involved in any part of the communication response. There are many ways to embed the plan into the work environment. Simply start by sharing it and explaining it to people and make it accessible on any shared computer systems. Share it not only with those inside the organization but, as mentioned, with those from other organizations who will need to be aware of the plan. Remember the stakeholder engagement plan that had to be developed as this can be utilized to assist the communication of the plan.

The next phase is to establish a rigorous and regular testing programme. This will not only ensure that the plan is fit for action but can also ensure there is a detailed working knowledge of the work by those briefed during the communication of the plan.

It is always challenging to find time in busy schedules to undertake scenario testing and exercising but these are essential ways to prepare and be ready to operate at speed when a crisis emerges. Think of it like a football team that needs to prepare for penalties. They are not always going to need to use the training on penalties but they never know when penalties could decide the match. Communicators will rarely face a crisis but when they do, everyone involved has to play their part and be at the top of their game. Training, exercising and planning for the potential crisis will keep you in a state of readiness.

When undertaking any kind of testing or exercising of the plan the key is to try to find the gaps that exist in the response and be open to the fact that things may not work effectively. That may sound like the wrong approach, but it is only by getting things wrong, identifying the gaps and highlighting delays that the plan can be developed to ensure it is fit and ready to be used when a crisis happens. Showing where the plans won't work will mean improvements can be made, so weaknesses can be seen as an opportunity.

Plans will have been developed using knowledge and possibly experience but even with experience they need to be tested and redesigned. This work will mean the paper version of the plan identifies the most effective and efficient way of working when a crisis breaks. Plans must be put through their paces in a real-life environment, allowing flaws to become clear. No organization wants to be wishing it had done more testing and exercising of plans in the aftermath of a crisis. Investing time ahead of a problem will save money and time when a crisis does happen and will also build the resilience of the business and team. Building resilience is an essential element for a successful response to a crisis. It can be done in two ways – with the individual and with the business. Resilience will improve the readiness and ability of people to respond to the crisis using the guidance, plans and procedures as well as equipping them to be confident and able to make decisions. Think of emerging issues as bricks that are picked up and placed in your rucksack; if you are resilient you can carry the rucksack without a problem but if you are under pressure some of the bricks need to be removed. Building resilience within the business will take some time to achieve if it doesn't already exist. The organizational culture must support the development of a resilient workforce. Systems and processes have a big part to play in creating a resilient organization, but are also linked to the culture and the 'feel' of the business. The CEO and top team are central to creating a culture within the organization that accepts failure as a learning opportunity. If plans, procedures and testing of them during 'normal' times is done in the right way then there will be a strong workforce ready to test and evaluate emergency plans.

Scenario testing and exercising can be done in several ways. Tabletop and desk-based exercises require a little planning but can be done very cost-effectively. Exercises that involve live role-playing are incredibly beneficial because they bring the element of reality but require resources in both planning and taking part in the exercise. These sorts of large-scale, real-life role-playing exercises are mainly undertaken by the military, government departments, law enforcement agencies and emergency services. However, they are now available for all communication teams using new software programmes and systems that can replicate the communication team environment in a realistic way. Live role-playing exercises often require volunteers to take parts such as playing the role of journalists or members of the public, so it is worth finding out if you are able to get involved in one of these exercises that is being carried out by another organization. If you can get involved then you will be able to see the elements working together, and how an exercise can be developed. Alternatively, work with specialist crisis communication agencies that can provide these services. You will undoubtedly take away learning that can be utilized for your own crisis communication planning and exercising.

Many organizations have testing procedures in place looking at high-risk areas. Those in food production, chemical handling and transportation will have testing regimes that will focus on the operational activity. It is a good starting point to test your crisis communication plan by adding the communication element into the planned operational activity. The scenario will already have been developed, which makes it easier to just add in the communication response as a real-time exercise without extensive work. Negotiate with the technical people who are responsible for these exercises and encourage them to make it even more realistic by adding a communication element to the testing. After all, no crisis or emergency will happen entirely out of the public gaze.

If there are no available exercises or tests planned, then you can run a communication-focused exercise. Look at the scenarios that you have outlined in the plan and identify which are the most likely to occur, such as cyberattack, service or product failure, and build a fictional desk-based scenario that will test the communication response. Securing the services of an external agency to assist in developing the exercise and testing plan can ensure it is undertaken thoroughly and with intense scrutiny. There are crisis communication and training companies operating worldwide that are experienced in this work. Having an independent review of your response and crisis communication plan is the only sure way of truly exposing any weaknesses. It eliminates any possible bias in evaluating the plan and response to testing as there is no personal attachment to the plan. It also gives an expert eye on the proposed approach you are detailing and means that you can have more confidence in the plans that have been developed.

Understand the plan

Exercising needs to be carefully developed so that it tests the right aspects of the plan. This means understanding where you may be vulnerable; again an external company or individual can undertake this when they are developing the test. Among the aspects that must be reviewed are the swift delivery of the initial alert to the issue or incident, the speed and quality of the early statements, the ability to respond to both media and social media issues, management of information as the situation develops and the ability to adapt the approach, statements and plan to reflect the changing nature of the crisis. The more detailed the exercise is the more you will be able to assess from the planned approach. If you have a full day or even two days, then the scenario can run as live time or almost live, which will ensure greater authenticity. However, even if you only have half a day you should be able to run a detailed tabletop exercise.

Ensuring the scenario is as real as possible for all those taking part is essential. It must feel as though the incident or issue is taking place, which will then mean that people act as they would if it was really happening. Running a media cell of pseudo-journalists who can ask questions as the scenario develops is hugely beneficial. They will operate as they would do reporting in the event of a crisis breaking and will ask the tough and challenging questions needed to test the ability to respond and adapt. Developing a test that includes a social media element has been problematic but in recent years several companies have developed systems that are able to operate crisis simulation and mimic the growth of a crisis in the digital space. This is a specialist area of work that is an essential ingredient in any exercise or scenario testing. Social media will be where most crises break or develop and having it included in your crisis communication plan and testing of the plan is non-negotiable.

Any exercise that is undertaken should involve key people from within the organization. The CEO, the department heads and all those who are identified as having a role to play within the crisis communication plan. The spokesperson, the people who support the workforce, the customer services staff – whoever has a part to play in communicating should take part in the test. If they are not able to take part in testing, at the very least they must clearly understand the plan and their role in delivering it. They need to know how the elements fit together, the structure, the sign-off process and the stakeholder engagement activity. Communicators have a key role to play in advising on the operational response, which we will explore in more detail in the following chapters.

The exercise increases its level of authenticity if you can involve key stakeholders and others who will be delivering parts of the communication response, or areas linked to the communication response. When an exercise is being developed to test the communication response alone and not, as mentioned earlier, as part of a wider operational scenario, consider who should be involved in the activity. If there are key regulatory bodies or agencies that are included in the stakeholder engagement section of the crisis communication plan, then consider how they may be able to take part in the exercise. It may also be beneficial to the stakeholder's development activity in this area to consider whether their plans are enough to be ready to respond to a crisis. Never be afraid to work alongside those you will need to be close to during a crisis. When something does happen, you will face similar challenges to those other agencies, which means you can often assist each other in the response. This may be by emphasizing statements, sharing information and keeping key individuals updated before they are asked to make a comment.

Where this is not considered possible because of sensitive issues, confidentiality or other organizational difficulties, the plan should at least have been discussed with communication colleagues from key stakeholder groups. Having a clear understanding of how different agencies and organizations will respond in the event of a crisis will help to build a consistent narrative and messaging. This consistency will assist both those affected and the wider public.

If there is a particularly well-developed and mature approach to risk and crisis management in the business, then you may feel able to involve the public, either as customers or service users. Provided they are well briefed about the scenario and what is expected of them they could deliver valuable insight into the intended approach and wording that will be used. This can also assist in building a diverse response and ensuring that the response is inclusive and accessible to groups. This will be covered in Chapter 6. This may be a step too far for many organizations though, so a safer alternative may be to use a focus group to discuss the plan and gather views about what the public would expect to happen publicly. If this is undertaken in an open way to strengthen the plan it could give a fully rounded and developed plan.

A crisis communication strategy must be regularly reviewed and continually developed. It cannot be written and then left on a shelf or in a section of the website for years. Organizations are regularly changing, developing and adapting. Every change within the organization requires the communication strategy and approach to be reconsidered. The same needs to happen with significant external environmental factors that can impact on the approach. For example, all crisis communication strategies and plans required reviewing and updating after the Covid-19 pandemic. The nature of work will change from year to year. There will be a different focus, a new CEO may bring different values, the environment may change with new building and new technology or new services and products may be introduced leading to new risks to the business. A crisis communication plan needs to be reviewed and assessed considering these changing circumstances so it can be amended and ready for action.

EXERCISING CHECKLIST

- Work with operational colleagues to develop an exercise if possible.
- Focus the exercise on the key areas of risk or approaches that feel weak.
- Consider bringing in an agency or third party to run the exercise.
- Decide whether you will do a full role-play exercise or a desk-based review.
- Involve key people from inside the organization to take part in, or run, the test.
- Discuss involvement in the exercise with communicators from key stakeholder organizations.
- Run a focus group with members of the public to test their response to the plan and any prepared messaging.
- Keep the plan under continual review, taking into account feedback from testing and changes in the organization and its operating environment.

CASE STUDY
Norway terror attack

On 22 July 2011 one man brought devastation to Norway. It started with a car bomb that was detonated in Regjeringskvartalet, the government quarter of Oslo. The bomb killed eight people and injured more than 200. Less than two hours later a second attack took place on the island of Utøya in Tyrifjorden where a Labour Party youth camp was being held. The lone-wolf terrorist, Anders Breivik, was dressed as a police officer and opened fire, killing 69 people and injuring more than 100, at least half of whom received serious injuries. The impact of the terror attacks was devastating, and the response of all the agencies to the attack was considered in detail in the Gjørv Report published in 2012.[2]

The extended timescale of the attack led to those caught up in the Utøya incident having the time to contact the outside world using social media, which was a place where the police and other agencies were noticeably absent.[3] This was problematic when the incident was unfolding on Facebook as well as Twitter. But the Gjørv Report did conclude that 'the Government's communication with the general public was good'.[4]

What improvements could be made?

The main issues were related to the failure to undertake enough and relevant exercising of the emergency plans and an inability to learn from the results and outcomes of what tests had been undertaken. The Report makes fascinating reading when considering how much time and effort to put into developing plans and then exercising them.

The Report concluded that 'Any failures were primarily due to:

- the ability to acknowledge risk and learn from exercises has not been sufficient;
- the ability to implement decisions that have been made, and to use the plans that have been developed, has been ineffectual;
- the ability to coordinate and interact has been deficient;
- the potential inherent in information and communications technology has not been exploited well enough;
- leadership's willingness and ability to clarify responsibility, set goals and adopt measures to achieve results have been insufficient.'

If crisis communications had been developed and reviewed by the key agencies involved, the weaknesses in their approach may have been identified. The relevant agencies should have also recognized the importance of social media to crisis communication. Developing more scenarios to test could have also highlighted the potential likelihood or risk of a firearms-related incident.

The Gjørv report underlined what should be remembered: 'The very essence of crisis management lies in the preparations: plans, drills, exercises, interaction and ways of thinking. Crisis management per se is a test of how well prepared one is.'

Key learning points

- Put enough time into testing, reviewing and developing your crisis communication plans.
- Help to create a culture of preparedness in dealing with any form of crisis.
- Expect the unexpected when developing the plan and think creatively about the scenarios you identify.

- Ensure you have factored in dealing with the media, social media, stakeholders and other key groups (more of this in the following chapters).

- Bring leadership of the organization into the discussions about the crisis communication plan and involve them in the testing.

- Develop a presence using the key channels of communication and prioritize them in the crisis communication plan.

- Build proactivity into your crisis communication plan so you can actively share the narrative and key messages.

CASE STUDY
Extreme weather and Storm Arwen

The end of 2021 and start of 2022 brought a number of extreme weather situations across Europe. One of the worst storms was in November 2021 when an extratropical cyclone brought strong winds and snow to parts of the UK, Ireland and France. Three people were killed and there were widespread power outages as winds reached up to 100mph.[5]

Hundreds of thousands of people were left without power, many of them for more than a week. For some people, it was up to 12 days before their power was restored.[6] In the UK, those most seriously affected were in the North East, Cumbria and Scotland. A major incident was declared in some areas but this didn't happen until some days after the storm had struck. The response led to military assistance being brought in.

In the aftermath the UK Government announced a review would take place looking at both the response and the way power companies communicated with customers. Ofgem, the industry regulator, announced it was to undertake its own review of the performance of network operators against the legal standards they are required to meet.[7] Those caught up in the impact of the storm and the aftermath shared their anger about the response. People talked of their despair and being in a nightmare where they were unable to wash, cook or keep warm. There were criticisms that the response from authorities was slow and it was not supported by a national effort linked to the Cabinet Office Briefing Rooms (COBR).[8]

Northumberland County Council declared a major incident a week after the storm, which was criticized as too late.[9,10] Northern Powergrid was criticized by customers for frequently changing its repair dates.[11] Regular communication took place on websites and social media but the challenge was that people did not have the power to access those channels.

Further environmental challenges occurred during the summer of 2022 when extreme temperatures affected Europe and other parts of the world. The weather highlighted operational challenges to how communities could manage situations. There were wildfires, and droughts were declared in many places.[12] It was clear during these unusual situations that there was a need for more preparation and explanation of what could be done to manage the situation. People were left hunting for information about what was best to do when temperatures soared. All of this information could have been shared as part of an ongoing discussion about how to be resilient and create resilient communities.

Key learning points

- Consider business continuity to ensure that there are methods of communication that can be used when extreme weather impacts on power. These business continuity plans should be in place for a range of risks.

- As well as honesty being important in crisis communication, so is managing expectations. People caught up in a crisis need to know what is happening, how things may develop, what to expect and what they can do to manage the situation.

- Clear messaging from all agencies involved in an emergency response is vital if it is to have the required impact and to assist people in understanding what they can do to support the response.

- Social media requires a detailed response and can be resource intensive. Crisis communication strategies must have dedicated sections outlining how social media will be managed during an incident. Cutting and pasting the same response to every query does not help to build confidence in the response. People need to feel their issues are being taken seriously.

- Start conversations about resilience when there is no emergency or crisis in place. People can become more comfortable with facing challenging situations if they know what they can do to be more prepared. This should be part of the consideration of crisis communication so there is a plan to explain how the business or organization will respond when something happens.

- Continually test your crisis communication plan. It doesn't matter how many times you have put the plan to the test, there is always more that can be done. With the development of communication and internal organizational developments the approach that is outlined may need to change.

Conclusion

Preparing to deal with a crisis and to ensure effective communication throughout is critical for every business and organization. It can help secure or mean the end of a brand that may be caught up in a serious incident or experiencing a significant issue. The starting point has to be ensuring that thinking has taken place to inform the creation of a crisis communication strategy and associated plans. It requires time and effort to be taken away from the daily business to consider what is required and how it will work alongside the organization's crisis response. Testing the response and the people involved in delivering it is a fundamental step in being crisis ready.

Alongside the strategy, develop a testing and exercising timetable that will put pressure on what you have developed to check whether it will meet the requirements of a crisis. Again, this will require time and resources but can mean the difference between having a plan that exists on paper and having one that has been stress tested to be ready for real-life implementation. Failing to take this approach in preparation will mean the plan is tested first in a real-life situation, which is not beneficial to the response or to the business.

Ensure that this preparatory work starts from the point of identifying and recognizing that a crisis is occurring through dealing with the incident and then working forward to implement the recovery phase. A crisis has the potential to exist and be in place for some time and to require careful communication and PR handling right through its lifetime and into the recovery phase. Work from the initial stages and document the communication requirements throughout the stages of the crisis. This work can then easily become the starting point to manage all types of crises.

Finally, sweating the small stuff really does matter. The crisis communication strategy has to provide the big elements such as the processes and procedures that will be in place, who will be the spokesperson, and how the narrative will be created and agreed. But it must also have associated plans and documents that can consider all the small aspects that have the potential to slow down or derail the communication response. Work from mapping the process through to making sure roles and responsibilities are clear. Ensure you have the appropriate IT devices and an emergency communication bag ready to be deployed. Make sure people know where the tools to manage the crisis are; if you have put time in to think things through then these small developments that are ready and available can save valuable time.

Notes

1 https://amecorg.com/amecframework/ (archived at perma.cc/AH92-VM6J)

2 A B Gjørv. Rapport fra 22. juli-kommisjonen, Departementenes Servicesenter, Oslo, 2012

3 E Frey. 'Do you tweet when your friends are getting shot?' Victims' experience with, and perspectives on, the use of social media during a terror attack, *Social Media + Society*, 2018, 4 (1). https://journals.sagepub.com/doi/full/10.1177/2056305117750715 (archived at perma.cc/5FSN-GKEZ)

4 A B Gjørv. Rapport fra 22. juli-kommisjonen, Departementenes Servicesenter, Oslo, 2012

5 ITV News. Storm Arwen: Three people die as gusts of wind of almost 100mph recorded in areas of UK (online video), 27 November 2021. www.youtube.com/watch?v=5jNUBKtKgnE (archived at perma.cc/FT27-BSXF)

6 BBC News Tyne and Wear. Storm Arwen: Homes without power for 12 days is 'best estimate', 1 December 2021. www.bbc.co.uk/news/uk-england-tyne-59516192 (archived at perma.cc/KJ9F-PNGA)

7 Ofgem. Storm Arwen Report, 9 June 2022. www.ofgem.gov.uk/publications/storm-arwen-report (archived at perma.cc/5UXZ-HA7A)

8 J Clinton. Storm Arwen: Thousands 'in despair' without power across North of England as residents criticize Government, *i News*, 5 December 2021. www.inews.co.uk/news/storm-arwen-thousands-without-power-snow-rain-forecast-1336162 (archived at perma.cc/5QJ8-YRXS)

9 Northumberland County Council. Storm Arwen – Major incident declared, 3 December 2021. www.northumberland.gov.uk/News/2021/Dec/Storm-Arwen-Major-Incident-declared.aspx (archived at perma.cc/5LCX-9JQS)

10 BBC News Tyne and Wear. Storm Arwen: Homes without power for 12 days is 'best estimate', 1 December 2021. www.bbc.co.uk/news/uk-england-tyne-59516192 (archived at perma.cc/KJ9F-PNGA)

11 BBC News Tyne and Wear. Storm Arwen: Northern Powergrid sorry for power cut communication, 4 December 2021. www.bbc.co.uk/news/uk-england-tyne-59531590 (archived at perma.cc/8Z5T-ATLR)

12 A Hancock. Almost half of Europe under drought warning conditions, *Financial Times*, 23 August 2022. www.ft.com/content/2c10693b-49f2-40db-a0c0-b46e3f706dbf (archived at perma.cc/SF6G-NC2M)

2

Recognizing a crisis: What it is and how to spot it

Crises arrive when you least expect them. They come in all shapes and sizes, from huge global events through to business-focused reputational issues. How they are categorized and viewed by an organization or business depends on the level of risk that it is prepared to carry. The scale of the crisis doesn't matter – if it is a crisis for the organization then it must be categorized as such. What is important is recognizing that you have a crisis on your hands before someone else tells you. This is the first fundamental step that has to be taken – admit that there is a problem. Being able to spot a crisis emerging is a skill but one that can be developed with some training and a bit of hard work. The key is understanding the anatomy of a crisis – what it is, how it looks and feels – and being able to dissect the parts that come together to create the crisis.

Risk managers, business continuity experts and lawyers may all stake a claim on being able to both recognize a crisis and provide the best advice for the business. But at best they provide only part of the answer and by the time a crisis has come to the attention of the legal team or the risk managers it is likely to have grown substantially and to be significantly advanced. This is where the role of the communicator comes in, with knowledge, experience and hopefully training that will enable them to take the lead. This chapter looks at how to recognize a crisis but will also cover the reasons why professional communicators are the ideal people to take a lead in identifying a crisis, making others aware and then galvanizing the business into action. A time of crisis is the time when a communicator who is prepared can step forward and demonstrate their worth to the organization. As mentioned in the previous chapter it is when the reputation of the communicator can be made or lost so being able to step up is essential.

What makes a crisis?

There are five elements that need to be in place to make the critical incident or issue into a full-blown crisis. First, this is a time of intense difficulty or, at the worst extreme, danger. Consider the natural disasters such as floods or the 2004 tsunami as well as the terrorist attacks that have taken place around the world. These are all incidents that clearly demonstrate extreme danger. But in other cases, such as the crisis Pepsi had with their advert in 2017, it can be classed as a time of intense difficulty for the brand. In short, a crisis must be serious and have an impact in some way whether that is on the business, on people, on the staff or on the environment.

Second, a crisis requires action to be taken. It is a point where difficult and important decisions must be made and puts the organization at a crossroads, a crisis point, where there may be a range of options available about how to respond. Those options will probably be forthcoming from departments including operations and human resources but almost definitely the legal team. The battle between legal and communications will be discussed in the next chapter. Myriad views about what should be done will be laid before the CEO but the role of the communicator can be key to a successfully managed crisis. Communicators have the ability to see across the organization and how it is positioned in the external environment.

Third, for the situation to be considered a crisis it must be a negative position, potential negative position or a negative change in the prevailing position of the company. There is no situation where a crisis will emerge that is seen in the early stages as a positive position for the business or organization. A positive approach can occur later if the crisis handling is effective and the opportunities that emerge during the crisis and in the recovery phase are taken forward. However, when the crisis emerges it will be seen negatively for the business.

Fourth, most crises develop abruptly and while a crisis may have been highlighted as part of the risk management process and planning, and considered within the scenarios, it is unlikely to have been recognized or identified before breaking. There will be little or no sign that the crisis is going to emerge. For example, during early 2020 there was an illness that was being identified but it became a crisis when the illness led to deaths and then restrictive measures had to be put in place. Alongside this it is possible that there were signs that could have alerted people to the developing storm but that they were just not recognized. Remember the tsunami; warnings were given but the scale of the incident was beyond what had been identified. In many reputational crises, which will be considered shortly, there may have been a complaint on social media, a letter to the business or a message given to frontline staff that was ignored, and the crisis then developed by virtue of the inaction. This is where the communicator has extra insight that can benefit the business because communication teams have a unique position. They can see across the business and beyond. They see what is happening in the environment around the organization.

Fifth and finally, the situation or issue must have an impact on people in some way. It can be argued that every action has an impact on someone somewhere at some point. However, a crisis will have a significant impact on people, their lives, communities, neighbourhoods and possibly even countries. It is this element of the human impact that can be forgotten in a world of share prices, business decisions and managing resources and yet, as Chapter 4 will show, it is the most important element within the response. If affected people are forgotten, then the crisis will grow and the opportunities to manage and repair the damage will be significantly hampered.

The five elements outlined will all be in place if your issue can be classified as a crisis. If these aspects are not in place, then you may have a serious or critical incident that you are attempting to manage. But it is important to remember that there are many significant and critical incidents that can be managed using the same crisis communication plan and approach that you develop. It may not require a full deployment of the crisis communication plan but the systems and processes that are in place will be beneficial in handling a serious incident.

TOP TIP

Every situation will be different and will have its own unique elements. Scenario planning, as outlined in Chapter 1, is important but it can never provide you with a script of how to deal with a crisis. To be successful in managing a crisis the communicator needs to have an open and enquiring mind. They need to be able to think on their feet, analyse data and situations quickly, ask the right questions to support their assessment and be prepared to think differently. A key part of this is to know the structure and processes that exist but to allow yourself some freedom of thought in testing and exercising the crisis communication plan.

Anatomy of a crisis

Crises can be categorized into two main groups – operational and reputational. The approach to managing them will be similar but it is essential in understanding the anatomy of a crisis to be able to distinguish between the two and to understand the characteristics of each group. Being able to analyse the crisis, understand the events that led up to it and see what differentiates it from other situations is critical to the formulation of the communication response and to developing a plan that will safely steer the business into the recovery phase.

Operational crises

An operational crisis is something that has happened in the environment around us because of either world events or a third party. It is a tangible event or situation that the business has been caught up in. This type of crisis, such as a fire, flood, health epidemic, other natural disaster, terrorist attack or riot, is often seen being dealt with by primary responders. It may involve a fundamental failure in the business processes such as a breakdown in the production line, contamination of products or failure in service delivery. In many situations the organization responsible will be at the heart of developing the response. It will be the organization's issue and leading on developing the narrative will be a matter for the business. But every brand, company or organization faces the possibility of being caught up in someone else's incident through association. With natural or manmade disasters, the location of them, the nature of them or the people involved in them may mean that the business is brought into the crisis. In the London Bridge terrorist attack in summer 2017 the company that had hired the vehicle used by the attackers was suddenly brought into the crisis. Questions were asked about what they did, what they knew and the level of their involvement. If not handled sensitively, carefully and with the principles of crisis communication at heart it could have produced a reputational crisis for the company involved.

Reputational crises

The second group is the reputational crises. The reputational crisis still has the same five elements that make it a crisis and the impact of it still could be the same, including loss of share price, impact on consumers, employees and communities. It still needs action to be taken to mitigate, manage and respond to the situation. But a reputational crisis does not need anything physically to have happened and it can be rooted in the feelings towards the organization, business or even an individual CEO. This type of crisis often breaks in the digital world with comments, events or issues emerging on social media. There is also the possibility that the crisis has been born from a media approach or position on the company or the way it is operating. A reputational crisis can involve the actions and behaviour of people within the organization. The employees may spark the events because of the way they work, the way they have acted or the way they have responded to circumstances. In the aftermath of the global financial crisis the record store HMV was in the position of making staff redundant when a disgruntled member of staff who had access to the company Twitter account began posting about what was happening, swiftly pushing the business into a situation where a crisis communication response was required. This highlights the importance of words and actions, bringing the two together and ensuring that the response puts people first.

The reputational crisis is rooted in perceptions. There is still the same potential impact as seen with an operational crisis, including loss of share price, loss of reputation, impact on consumers, employees and wider communities. But for a reputational crisis to emerge there does not need to have been anything that has physically happened. We live not only in the real world but in a virtual world and brands and businesses must be able to deal with crises that happen in both. With the growth of social media and the digital platforms that exist there is every opportunity for people to publish and broadcast their own views about any situation, incident, issue and – most importantly for communicators – organizations. People can post if they are unhappy about services or products. They can highlight if they believe there has been inappropriate behaviour or corruption from the business. They can challenge where they feel something should not have happened or where something should have happened that didn't.

They can give their personal story, which has the potential to elevate even the most mundane issue into a national or international media storm. If the impact on the individual is seen as particularly severe or creating unnecessary difficulties, then public sympathy will feed the social media and media response, quickly spiralling the situation into a full-blown reputational crisis. The actions of the organization, whether it is swift to respond or slow and uncaring, can define whether the situation develops from a small problem into a crisis. It is important to recognize that this type of crisis builds and is fed by perceptions – first from those involved and then from the wider public, community and society. It starts from the actions and behaviour of the people within the business, and for those working inhouse as a communicator within the business it can be challenging to identify this kind of crisis emerging. Critical to this response is being prepared for an attack on the reputation of the business through planning and testing, which we covered in Chapter 1. Having insight into the business, what people think of it, how its reputation stacks up in the marketplace and what the frontline service looks like is essential to being able to identify this crisis emerging. If a communicator is in the dark about what the perception of the business is and what could be classified as normal, then they will not be able to assist in providing the business with an early warning of a reputational crisis. We will discuss this further later in this chapter when we consider what the role of the communicator should be.

Of course, this freedom and access for people to publish individual views does present the opportunity for fake news to rear its head. Fake news is misinformation that often is deliberately created to negatively impact on a scenario, events or potentially businesses. It can range from sensationalizing a set of circumstances through to fabrication of events. Primarily, fake news exists in the digital and social media world, but it can leach out into the more traditional mainstream news media. Communicators must be alert to the possibility that the issue and the views that are being shared are being developed for another purpose, which is to discredit or negatively impact on the business. This may sound Machiavellian and highly unlikely to be experienced by most communicators, but this is a very real threat to brands and organizations. It is why an open mind and attention to the detail of what is happening or being said is critical to the crisis communicator. The development of fake news within a crisis situation creates an additional issue or crisis that needs to be managed. It means the communicator is effectively having to manage two situations. First, leading the response to the crisis itself and the communication that is required, and second managing the potential reputational damage that could be caused by fake news starting to circulate. Dealing effectively with fake news is not easy, and is something we will cover in Chapter 3 when we consider the operational response.

CASE STUDY
United Airlines

On 9 April 2017 a United Airlines flight sparked a social media storm that developed quickly into a reputational crisis. Flight 3411 out of Chicago had been overbooked and airline employees had offered vouchers to passengers in an attempt to get them to leave the flight. None of the passengers accepted the vouchers and so four passengers were selected to be removed from the flight involuntarily. One passenger refused to give up his seat when requested and security staff were called to forcibly remove him from the plane. Video of the incident was recorded by passengers on the flight, which was then posted on social media and quickly went viral. Criticism of the incident and the behaviour of the airline was swift and came from the highest levels of government.

The next day the CEO issued a statement, which read:

> This is an upsetting event to all of us here at United. I apologize for having to reaccommodate these customers. Our team is moving with a sense of urgency to work with the authorities and conduct our own detailed review of what happened. We are also reaching out to this passenger to talk directly to him and further address and resolve this situation (Oscar Munoz, CEO, United Airlines).[1]

The language lacked humanity and appeared to justify the forcible removal, when video that was circulating showed the passenger hit his head on an armrest as he was dragged from the flight. Behind the scenes the CEO sent an email to United Airlines staff that appeared to support the behaviour of the staff and criticize the passenger for failing to quietly comply with the request. This internal message was circulated outside the organization and was covered by the media and on social media. It was not until two days later that the apology was finally given and a more contrite statement provided that said a review would be undertaken. On 11 April the airline's parent company saw almost $1 billion lost from its market value and while the apology did lead to some recovery the value was still down by $250 million.[2]

Analysing the response

The incident broke on social media and the communication team should have spotted it swiftly and been able to provide insight about the impact it was having on reputation and confidence in United Airlines. An effectively trained and prepared communicator would have advised the CEO to take a different approach from the start. Regardless of processes and procedures the video appeared brutal and the action would never be justifiable in the minds of passengers and the general public. The communicator could have tackled the wording and ensured it was more human and sensitive to the public mood. They could have also ensured an apology was provided, a sympathetic narrative created and pushed the CEO to meet with the aggrieved passenger to demonstrate action being taken.

The definitive response from the business on the events was slow to emerge. It was two days after the incident when the CEO finally said sorry and that a review would be carried out. This had led to difficult media interviews that had to be undertaken in an attempt to claw back some confidence from the public. Once this response was provided it did limit some of the damage to reputation as the business had recognized there was an issue, that it was unacceptable and that the business would review and learn from this situation.

Key learning points

- Monitor social media and be able to alert the executive team to criticism or concern.
- Reputational crises can have a significant impact on the business, including its share price and market value.
- Ensure a speedy response to avoid the situation running ahead on social media.
- Develop statements sensitive to the public view of what has happened.
- Gather the facts as quickly as possible and ensure honesty in the response.
- Work alongside the CEO or company spokesperson from the first alert to a crisis ensuring coordination of all communication – internal, external and stakeholders.
- Communication can be the glue to the response by supporting the senior team and providing advice alongside legal and HR to develop a response acceptable to the public.

The importance of preparedness

It is vital that any organization or business has a system in place to identify risks in all aspects of its work. The risks can come from processes, staffing, stakeholders or other operational activity but ensuring there is a way to capture them and consider appropriate mitigation is essential. It should be part of the business planning process and be considered from the highest levels of the organization. No CEO should be ignorant of the risks that the business they lead may face. The role of the CEO in leading the response to the crisis was discussed in the previous chapter, which recommended their involvement in the development of crisis communication plans. However, they may delegate the responsibility to a company spokesperson. The risk management process sits alongside the crisis response plans and has a place in every section of the business. Communicators have a key role to play in developing the risk management approach but they may not lead on it if in a larger organization where there is likely to be a team to undertake this work.

Risk management is a detailed business that requires analysis and evaluation.

There are five stages to considering risks:

1 Understand the business context

2 Identify the risks

3 Assess the risk

4 Evaluate the risk and the possible impact it could have on the business

5 Establish the mitigation to prevent or minimize the risk

Communicators need to have understood the risks of the business to assist in the development of the crisis communication plan. The risks are likely to be where situations emerge that can grow into a crisis. But as well as understanding these business risks, communicators also need to be able to highlight reputational risks. As we have seen, the likelihood of a reputational crisis occurring is high.

The process may involve the development of a risk management matrix or communication-focused risk management plan. Any system that is introduced needs to fit seamlessly into the organization's approach to risk and this approach needs to support the role of the communicator in this work. The starting point must be a full understanding of the risks that may occur or impact on the business. List all of these and have a clear assessment of what they each mean to the organization. Compiling this from all the sections, departments or units within the business will provide the most comprehensive list of risks. It may help to take a systematic approach that follows each of the stages of production or service delivery within the business to break down the threats and risks for each section. Alternatively, you could just ask each department and unit within the business to provide a list of the risks they face. Once you have the comprehensive list of risks the next stage is to consider the potential impact, both operational and reputational, and the likelihood of the risk emerging. This can be done on a scored or a low, medium and high basis. But it will mean a final rating that gives the hotspots of risk within the business. Undertaking the analysis to achieve the final rating can be done using a variety of scoring methods so review which may be most appropriate.

The key stage in the whole process is working out the mitigation that can be undertaken to prevent the risk appearing, developing and building into a crisis. Take all the highest risks identified in the scoring and look at what can be done to stop them happening. For example, if one of the risks is about the failure of a manufacturing process then the mitigation would be to have a maintenance programme in place to keep the machinery serviced. This is not within the remit of the communicator but does highlight the thought process that needs to be in place. For the reputational risks the communicator should take a lead in deciding the mitigation that needs to be in place. Consider the likely risk of a disgruntled employee making a negative comment about the business on social media; the mitigation may be to boost the internal communication activity and employee engagement. It may also include a comprehensive social media monitoring system being put in place to act as an early warning to such posts. Outlining the risks and mitigation is a detailed process and while it is labour intensive it requires much less time to monitor and maintain once it is in place. A quarterly review of the risks to understand what may have been reduced or increased in potentiality alongside a consideration of the mitigation and how it has developed will assist in the long-term development or preparedness for both individuals and the organization. It keeps the corporate mindset focused on preparing for a crisis, which is part of the battle towards developing an effective crisis communication response.

FIGURE 2.1 Example of communication-focused risk management plan

Risk	Implications	Impact	Mitigation	Rating
Website failure	Possible attack or IT breakdown that takes the website down	Lack communication channel and possible sales	Comprehensive security plan to undertake penetration testing, and have a back-up ready to use. Final option is to focus on messaging through social media channels	
Mixed messaging	Frontline staff providing inaccurate or inappropriate information to customers/service users	Impact on sales or customer confidence	Staff communication plan in place with checklist in crisis communication plan to ensure first to receive accurate information and updates	
Stakeholder complaint	Key individual or agency complaint about the operation of the business	Damage confidence of other stakeholders and/or customers	Robust public affairs strategy in place with support of CEO and management team	
Response is slow to issue	Slow messaging that will leave people making their own assessment of the situation	Impact on confidence in the business and on the trust in communication	Develop process for managing alert to communication and for sharing of updates. Ensure CEO and senior management team understand the process and are supportive.	

Total IT failure			
Factory breakdown			
Customer complaint			
Online troll			
Cyberattack			

The likelihood is rated as unlikely as green ☐, possible as amber ☐ and likely as red ▉. The impact is rated as low impact green, moderate impact amber, severe or critical impact red. The final assessment will take into account any mitigation that is in place with the impact always as the dominant assessment as in the example above.

For a full-colour version of this figure, visit www.koganpage.com/CCS and download it from the Supporting resources tab.

Getting prepared is a fundamental step to achieving the best possible response to a crisis whenever it emerges. This was outlined in Chapter 1 with the details of the importance of testing and scenario planning in creating the crisis communication plan. It is not enough for communicators to be prepared for a critical incident – the whole business must be prepared for the unexpected. There are many ways of getting people ready to respond to a crisis. Within the communication team, who will be involved, it is essential that everyone is aware of the risks within the risk matrix and, more importantly, the mitigation that has been identified. Share the information and allow people to discuss and consider what the risks and mitigation mean. It will assist them with the regular communication activity and mainstreaming the work required to minimize the risk. We can see in the example of the requirement to increase employee engagement that the communication team have a key part to play. Regular team and individual meetings should highlight the risks, responses and crisis plan. It may be worth considering having a pre-risk plan that exists to cover the situations and issues that the communication team have recognized could grow to become a reputational risk. It would be a potential critical incident list or possible crises list. The more people involved in thinking about the issues and considering the response that will be required, the easier it will be when a problem or crisis emerges because they are already conversant with the language of the crisis.

A team that is trained and prepared can provide both strategic and tactical guidance when faced with a crisis. No team can operate at the peak of its ability and capability as required during a crisis if it has not prepared, developed and honed its approach. It may appear to be time that is not boosting productivity in any way but this is not the case. This work can build an effective team, can increase resilience and will assist in developing the team to be able to start thinking strategically and not just focusing on the tactics of communication. The investment, while ultimately preparing and ensuring readiness for a crisis, can support development of the communication team and build the required culture of learning.

The organization's approach should be to have a regular risk management meeting where key heads of sections of the business such as legal, operational, customer service, HR, finance and communication come together to consider the matrix and the mitigation. This is also a valuable opportunity to consider the crisis communication plan and highlight the roles that individuals need to play in the response. It may be that the communicator needs to drive this development work being put in place and to provide details of the potential benefits to the bottom line of the business if a crisis is effectively managed. Sharing examples of where organizations have grown or shrunk because of the way risks and a crisis were managed will support the argument for moving risk management and crisis preparedness up the corporate agenda. If preparedness is not in place, then the communicator should use influencing skills to put it on the agenda. It is important to remember the value of the testing and exercising of planning for a crisis, and together with the risk management work it becomes a complete package to support the business.

The role of the communicator

Communication teams have a unique position in any organization. They are one of the only parts of the business that can see everything that goes on, mainly because it is their role to find the positive stories to share and the problems that may need to be managed. Other than the CEO and top team, no other department has this panoramic understanding. Communication leads should operate as special advisers to the CEO daily and if this is in place it makes advising during a crisis a much easier role to step into. There are five key roles that a communicator can take in the preparation phase when developing a crisis communication approach:

1 Communicators can support the development of organizational strategy.

2 Communicators can be a critical friend to the CEO faced with leading the crisis response.

3 Communicators can provide an early warning system to potential crises.

4 Communicators can guide the business in establishing processes.

5 Communicators can be the glue that holds together the crisis response.

If we look at each of these in turn, we can see the skills, experience and knowledge that are required to allow the communicator to operate in these roles.

Communicators can support the development of organizational strategy

Earlier in this chapter the importance of a risk management process was outlined. It is this system that can be the foundation for the whole approach that is taken to deal with possible negative issues and events that could impact on the business. As we have seen, the communicator has a key role within this work and if required should step in to support the integration of a process within the business. This effort, while not strictly a communication responsibility, will benefit the communication team in the long run and support corporate development activity. It is an investment for the future when having considered the risks, developed the mitigation and created the appropriate plans. The whole organization can then use the work to move quickly into crisis response mode. It is with this work that the communicator steps into being able to support the development of organizational strategy and is seen as a critical strategic function to the business. It is essential to remember that a key part of the organizational strategy development and the successful long-term operation of the business is creating a risk management process and a crisis plan.

Communicators can be a critical friend to the CEO faced with leading the crisis response

We have already seen in the previous chapter that the role of the CEO is critical in the response phase of managing the crisis. Being the face of the response to the crisis and being the CEO at a time of a critical issue or incident can be a very lonely place. They need to have tactical advisers around them who can provide them with enough information about the options for the response that will allow them to make the appropriate operational and reputational decisions. The communication lead has a role to play in sitting alongside the CEO to provide them with instant advice on the approach to take and how decisions may impact on people and their views of the crisis. The communication lead can also help them personally to ensure they can offer support to staff and be visible in the communication activity. Decisions made about the operational response could impact on the reputation of the business and the communicator can be the critical friend giving the view of the action before it is taken. For example, if the business decides not to recall a product that may be of poor quality then the communicator can highlight the impact on reputation this decision can have and the possible loss of confidence. No decision that is made about the response to the crisis will be without an impact in some way on the confidence people have in the organization and ultimately on the communication. The communicator can highlight the actions that are more likely to protect or boost reputation or minimize the damage to the business. It is also important to consider the consequences of actions and activities that are going to be implemented. To be able to assume this position as a critical friend or tactical adviser during a crisis, the communication lead must have developed a positive working relationship with the CEO and senior management team in the quieter times.

Communicators can provide an early warning system to potential crises

Communication teams and individuals providing support to businesses should have systems in place for regularly monitoring and reviewing media and social media reporting about the organization. They should know the views of the customers or service users and carry out regular reputation monitoring. If this work is underway then the communicator should be able to chart any changes that may require mitigation action, or identify criticism or negative commentary that has the potential to escalate. As mentioned, a risk management process within the business provides an avenue to raise these concerns. However, it is important to remember that issues can happen at any point, and speed of response, as we will go on to see, is essential to a positive result. Always take the opportunity to high-light an issue of concern and don't assume that someone will already have made the senior team aware.

Communicators can guide the business in establishing processes

Systems and processes form an essential framework to crisis management. Investing time to ensure risk management, business continuity and crisis management are within the business' DNA is critical. If these elements are not in place or being discussed within the business then it is something that a communicator can change. They can highlight the potential impact of failing to manage a crisis on aspects including share prices, customer confidence and even recruitment into the business. After all, working in an organization that has been heavily criticized because of poor crisis management will not be attractive to potential employees. Being able to use data, insight and experiences taken from organizations that have been through crises provides a convincing narrative to share with the executive team. Once you have gained support, then as a communicator you can help shape the framework to ensure it gives maximum support to the essential aspects of communication and reputation management during a crisis.

Communicators can be the glue that holds together the crisis response

One thing that communicators are very good at is working quickly, gathering data, analysing situations and developing responses. It is these skills that can come to the fore when an issue or incident emerges. Communication takes a leading position when a crisis happens. Managing reputation is essential to a successful outcome for the business. This means that the communicator who is equipped and prepared can step forward and be the lynchpin holding everything together. In being able to provide the most appropriate communication response you must understand the issue or incident and what it means for all involved or affected. You must understand the organizational response. You must be able to understand the possible stages of the crisis and how it may develop. This means a strong position can be taken at the centre of the crisis response. The situation presents an opportunity for the communicator to be the glue that holds the crisis response together by helping to guide the operational activity and identifying any weaknesses. This may sound fanciful but it is achievable if the planning and preparatory work has been undertaken and the organization is effectively in a state of readiness.

The role of the communicator can move way beyond that of merely being the writer of a statement, supporting media interviewees and responding to social media commentary. In being able to see the bigger picture across the business they are moving to a strategic position, making the communication function as a part of the boardroom discussion. Communicators need to be trained and ready to take up this opportunity and position when a crisis emerges. It is stepping outside of the comfort zone of the usual remit of communication but will demonstrate the value of the communication team's work for many years to come.

Previously we have discussed the training required for members of the communication team and those who will be involved in the response. Further professional development is required to ensure readiness to step up and offer both a strategic and a tactical response to the crisis. All communicators are advised to have continuous professional development plans to support them throughout their working life. This should cover both practical and behavioural skills. The individual and their line manager where applicable should identify areas of weakness that require improvement and areas of positive development to continue to grow. Within this discussion about personal development, crisis communication skills must be considered.

The skills required to take a strategic position in response to a crisis range from negotiating and influencing skills, understanding behavioural change communication insights, systems thinking, data analysis and leadership development through to resilience and understanding risk management. All these skills will support the general communication activity that takes place every day but will be hugely beneficial during a time of crisis. The CEO must have confidence that the communication team and the lead communicator within the business are ready to support the organization, the CEO and the company spokesperson in the event of a crisis. And more than that they have to be confident that the communication team will be operating at their most effective throughout the crisis, including into the recovery phase.

CASE STUDY
Cyberattack on Canadian authorities

In August 2020 a number of Canadian Government departments were subjected to a cyberattack. On 15 August there were reports of a breach of the Canada Revenue Agency (CRA) and the Government of Canada Key service (GCKey), the departments responsible for benefit payments.[3] The attempts to log in to accounts happened just over a week earlier on 7 August but it was only on 15 August that a decision was made to suspend accounts. The Royal Canadian Mounted Police were informed of the attack on 11 August.[4]

It was estimated more than 11,000 accounts were hacked in an attack believed to be caused by using stolen usernames and passwords. The practice is called 'credential stuffing', which is when details stolen in previous attacks are used.[5]

Media reports criticized the CRA, as people said they were unable to contact it and had been waiting for details of what they should do. One person claimed in a report to have had account details changed without their knowledge as early as May although this could not be definitively linked to the same attack. The system was finally back up and running on 19 August according to the CRA Twitter account, @CanRevAgency.[6]

A statement released by the Chief Information Officer of Government Canada had little recognition of the disruption and impact that the attack had on people.[7] Instead it focused on the technical aspects of the breaches and the issue of passwords being reused, which may have appeared to be 'victim blaming'.

Key learning points

- Ensure out-of-hours cover – this situation broke at a weekend and instead of providing information immediately, the first announcements were at a press conference organized on the Monday. Crisis communication needs a quick response no matter whether it is at the weekend or overnight.

- Monitor social media for signs of issues and concerns that may link to a crisis situation – people who tried to make contact with the agencies over the weekend had to wait until the working week to be given important information.

- Explain quickly what people need to do and provide some reassurance – in this situation involving finances and personal data there would always be a high level of concern about what had happened.

- Know your risks and be prepared for them – cyberattacks are a continuous threat for all businesses, organizations and individuals. Being able to respond quickly is important and work could have been put in place to have a cyber crisis communication plan ready to implement.

- Avoid blaming those caught up in the crisis – it will always be received negatively if communication appears to criticize those who have been impacted by the crisis. Focus on using positive language that focuses on what is being done to support people.

- Don't be too technical or use jargon or acronyms in crisis communication – the information needs to be as clear as possible and should be focused on helping the people affected. It is important to focus on what matters, and that is the people, what they need to do and how they are being supported.

Conclusion

Effective communication first requires the communicator to understand what makes a crisis and to feel confident that they can identify one as it starts to emerge. Being able to do this will provide valuable time in which to start to act either to avert or be ready to respond to the crisis. Developing this skill can take time but there are training courses available. One of the best ways to develop your own crisis identification abilities is to watch and learn from other organizations. Look at what they do the moment a crisis emerges and ask them after it has concluded. This will be easy to achieve as communication is instant and will immediately mean discussion on social media and extensive media coverage. It doesn't matter whether it is an international issue or one affecting a region of a country, the discussion will take place on relevant forums.

Preparation is key to the effective delivery of a crisis communication strategy. No one can start to learn about crisis communication or develop the plan when they are faced with an emerging situation.

Investing time now will bring rewards when reputational issues occur or when a crisis hits.

At the heart of the preparation work is making sure, as a communicator, you understand the risk management approach and systems of the business you are working with. It may feel a long way away from the work of the communicator but it has a direct impact on the crisis response. Take an interest in the risk register that documents the potential risks the business may face and the mitigation that is in place. Use this data to inform the crisis communication planning and testing as it provides valuable information. Develop your own communication-focused risk register of possible critical issues, incidents or events that can impact on the reputation of the business.

If you have an understanding of what makes a crisis, and of what the risk management approach is, then you are more likely to be able to deal with issues that emerge to ensure that they don't develop to become crises. Be clear how you can escalate concerns and where they need to be raised in the business to put activities in place to minimize the chance of a full-blown crisis situation. The communicator has an important role to play in any organization and needs to step up and demonstrate leadership in managing a crisis.

Notes

1 Associated Press. Read United CEO's 3 statements on passenger dragged off flight, Boston.com, 11 April 2017. www.boston.com/travel/business/2017/04/11/read-united-ceos-3-statements-on-passenger-dragged-off-flight (archived at perma.cc/ZHY8-J764)

2 I Kottasova. United loses $250 million of its market value, *CNN Business*, 11 April 2017. https://money.cnn.com/2017/04/11/investing/united-airlines-stock-passenger-flight-video/ (archived at perma.cc/KZC8-HGY5)

3 R P Jones. Cyberattacks targeting CRA, Canadians' COVID-19 benefits have been brought under control: officials, CBC News, 17 August 2020. www.cbc.ca/news/politics/cra-gckey-cyberattack-1.5689106 (archived at perma.cc/L69A-WQLE)

4 P Newton. Cyberattack shuts down Canadian government accounts, including those delivering COVID assistance, CNN Business, 17 August 2020.

www.edition.cnn.com/2020/08/17/tech/cyberattack-canada-government-accounts/index.html (archived at perma.cc/L546-V2KB)

5 G La-douceur Despins. Cyber attacks: Several Canadian government services disrupted, WeLiveSecurity, 24 August 2020. www.welivesecurity.com/2020/08/24/cyber-attacks-canada-revenue-agency-government/ (archived at perma.cc/UVM7-8KAH)

6 @canrevagency, August 2020

7 Government of Canada (2020) Statement from the Office of the Chief Information Officer of the Government Canada on recent credential stuffing attacks, 15 August 2020. www.canada.ca/en/treasury-board-secretariat/news/2020/08/statement-from-the-office-of-the-chief-information-officer-of-the-government-canada-on-recent-credential-stuffing-attacks.html (archived at perma.cc/7Q54-XBGH)

3

The operational response: The approaches and how they relate to communications

The action that the organization or business takes to deal with the events that have taken place is central to every crisis. No amount of carefully crafted words or proactive communication strategies will provide an effective response if the business is not seen to take appropriate action. This is where the communication professional can be crucial, providing strategic advice and assessing the way the action taken will be viewed. The communicator provides valuable insight into the impact action may have on reputation. Later in this chapter we will discuss why protecting reputation should not be the sole purpose of both operational work and communication activity when dealing with a crisis.

In the previous chapter we discussed how to identify a crisis and the role that communication teams and individuals can play in being an early warning system to recognize a possible problem in the early stages of its development. However, despite all the effort to prepare and mitigate risks a crisis can still occur and it is the actions in the first few minutes, first hour and first day that will either put you in a place where you can move forward and deal positively with events, or you will be under consistent pressure that negatively impacts on the business. If you have done the work we have discussed then you will have been prepared with a crisis communication plan that is clearly linked to the business objectives. This was covered in detail in

Chapter 1. It is in the moments when a crisis emerges that this plan will become a vital support to those dealing with the communication response. It provides some structure and resilience to what will be a chaotic situation. When you are called on to implement a plan at short notice, having done all the preparatory work will lessen the stress.

There are many skills that are required to deliver successful crisis communication but the most important is being able to remain calm under pressure. Being prepared can help people with this as they both have a framework and know the framework for dealing with events. A calm and assured appearance from the chief communicator dealing with a crisis will help to reassure the CEO, whoever is the spokesperson for the issue and the senior managers. It is a sense of calm that can spread to others dealing with the crisis. But in that sense of calm there should also be humanity and empathy. This is a point where leaders should not be hysterical, but neither should they appear to be completely devoid of emotion. When we are calm and unflustered, we can have a clear approach to the decision-making process and will be able to define the right steps with cool logic. This cool and calm signifies the resilient organization that we outlined in Chapter 2.

The first steps

Early alert

The alert that a crisis has taken place can come from many parts of the business. It may be that the operational team spot an issue, or that the human resources staff have identified a problem, or that the legal team have uncovered something, or as discussed earlier that the reputation monitoring from the communication team has identified an issue. The key is that no matter which section recognizes the problem the CEO and senior leaders will be the ones to declare that this is a crisis or critical incident for the business. Later in this chapter we will see how the military and emergency services have a very clear process for declaring a critical incident, which then sets off a chain of events to put in place the actions that are required. This formal and structured approach provides useful guidance and advice in managing a crisis for all businesses.

In declaring that there is a crisis taking place the organization should then have a structured approach that it moves into, which will ensure that action is taken and that all the departments involved in the response have been alerted to the situation. This ensures a representative from each section of the business will receive an alert that puts them in a state of readiness. It also triggers the activation of the crisis or emergency plans. This can easily be done using mobile technology that allows one message to be received by the key group of senior leaders. You could use text messages, a WhatsApp group or a product that has been bought by the company to send the message. The key is to find something that can reach people quickly and with the minimum fuss. During the 2020 Covid-19 pandemic the ability to communicate quickly with all employees became essential. Staff needed to receive updates on where, when and how to undertake their work and in many cases could not be allowed into their place of work. Having systems in place that will provide critical updates directly to employees is a key part of business continuity plans.

Each leader can then refer to their crisis plan and start to implement it, as well as identifying where adaptation of the outline plan may be required. The communicator should be among the first to receive the alert to a crisis. The most vital thing in dealing with a crisis is ensuring a swift response to what has happened is communicated. The organization must be seen publicly to be aware of the issue and be working on dealing with it at the earliest possible opportunity. If you imagine a system outage for a tech provider or the failure of banking systems, there is often significant criticism in the early stages because the business does not recognize there is an issue and customers are left in the dark, unclear what is happening. It may be that the first the business knows of a problem is when it is being openly discussed on social media, and in many cases will have built up a head of steam with comments from irate customers. This can all be avoided if communicators can work quickly and have built a plan that allows them to act swiftly on behalf of the business without having to deal with many layers of approvals. There had been an acceptance of a 'golden hour' during which it was essential to both recognize that the crisis had occurred and get the first communication out to both staff and the public. But due to technological developments, media and the rise of social media this is now a 20-minute window. There is just 20 minutes to alert communication teams to a situation emerging and to say something publicly and to staff. This situation makes it essential to pre-plan, develop and agree short statements that can be used immediately.

Checklists

In Chapter 1 there was an example of a checklist for the crisis communication plan that outlined the initial activity that should be undertaken. All the very first actions will be focused on having a clear situational update from those dealing with the problem. As a communicator you must understand what information is available and how accurate it is, what information is not currently known and what the potential outcomes to the situation could be. You can then add to this with your own knowledge of the public view of the issue and the reputational impact that may already be known in the early stages. In addition, any historical awareness of the business, risks and previous issues is helpful at this stage. This detailed knowledge and understanding means the communicator can outline what can be said in the narrative response and that it can be done quickly while still being honest and reassuring. At its centre it must focus on what is known at that moment in time and allow the communication and conversation to develop as more details become known. It can then be followed by a plan of what information can be released, key times in the operational response, essential information that is required and preparing so that future developments can take place. Getting the maximum amount of information about the developing situation is needed even when the situation may still be unclear. Gather as much of the factual detail as you can.

Getting the facts

Communicators may worry that there is little about the crisis that is clear, as in the example of the banking system failure. In that case the bank may not know what has caused the problem or how long it may take to rectify, which is a challenge to effective communication. However, there are lots of points that can be made. First, a swift statement that recognizes there is a problem and talks about action being taken will help to reassure people that the business is aware and dealing with things. In the early stages of a crisis this is essential. But other details about the scale of the team responding, the alternative arrangements that may be in place for customers and how people can get updates are all elements that should be able to be shared when information is scarce. Always ask why you can't release information rather than whether you should, as this helps to create an open and transparent approach.

The checklist in Chapter 1 mentions having a 'grab bag' with all the vital information the first communicator needs, and this will assist if the communication team need to respond from a venue other than their normal working base. Again, in the very first moments of a crisis happening, the lead communicator needs to be sat alongside the operational leaders developing the approach and coaching the CEO or senior leader who may be the spokesperson even if this is done remotely. Being involved in the initial discussions about the operational action required will ensure that the communicator can input into the decision making. Reputational concerns can be raised and if action is likely to be perceived negatively this information can be provided to ensure that the CEO is aware of all the relevant advice to support decision making.

Writing the plan

Once you have made an initial statement, have gathered as much information as possible about the situation and have started to develop the crisis communication plan, then consideration should be given to starting the stakeholder engagement. Making a swift connection to those stakeholders most critical to the business will bring long-term benefits. It ensures they have information before or at least at the same time as the wider public and if they are approached for their comment by the media or via social media they will have a knowledgeable position to speak from. In this early stage, getting the public messages and situational update to all employees is also vital to effective crisis communication. We will learn more about this in Chapter 4, looking at the affected people, and Chapter 7, looking at wellbeing and resilience as part of the crisis communication response. Employees should always be given information before it becomes public so that they are fully aware of the position and what the message is. This helps to make it easier to develop a shared narrative about the issue and the events that followed.

Gathering support

On a more practical note, the first few hours after a crisis has been identified and work is underway to provide a coherent and consistent response across the business is also an important time to set some processes underway that will assist in the future management of communication. First is the importance of recognizing the resources that are required to provide the effective response to the incident or event from the communication team. As outlined in Chapter 1, there may be a range of people you call in to support communication in the hours, days and weeks that follow the crisis erupting. The wheels need to be set in motion to ensure that this resourcing is in place to boost the communication response and that there are sufficient people to run 24 hours a day if required and to be able to cover all the roles and responsibilities detailed in the crisis communication plan.

The first one to five hours can be managed by a core group of staff, depending on the scale of the crisis, but as time goes on more actions need to be undertaken, more information needs to be shared, and this sharing is fundamental to an effective communication response. Never underestimate the speed with which a crisis can develop and the number of people that you need to be able to manage the communication strategy. Second, don't forget to have a logging system in place that notes what you have released publicly, what decisions have been made and any authorizations that have been given and by whom.

This should be accessible to the team providing the communication response so they are clear about what questions can be answered both in the media and on social media, and that they are aware of when updates will be available. You can do this through a shared drive or Google Docs depending on the internal security systems that are in place to protect documents. In the aftermath of the issue or incident the action that has been taken will be subject to review of some kind and being able to provide a clear narrative about the communication activity, what was done and why will be hugely beneficial. If you attempt to do this retrospectively then you will find it difficult to accurately recall what was done and at what point. Logging may seem very basic but without it the consistency of the narrative can easily be lost as more people are involved in supporting the communication response.

The initial statement

The first communication that comes from the business about the crisis is the most critical. As mentioned, if it sets the scene in the right way it can increase the probability of an effective outcome once the crisis is concluding. It can maintain reputation and public confidence and support the viability of the business. Make sure the statement shows an awareness of the situation and states that action is being taken. It should also give an indication that more information will be provided as things develop. This means the first statement does not need to be extensive and detailed, but releasing it quickly will provide some time to allow the communicator to get the full situational update. It leaves the way open for more information to come to light and avoids stating information that may prove to be assumption or inaccurate.

FIGURE 3.1   Example of a logging system

SOURCE Reproduced with permission of Christine Townsend, MusterPoint CEO (17 November 2019)

TOP TIP

The process for approving statements when dealing with a crisis needs to be as lean as possible so the fewest possible number of people are involved. Why is this? It is to speed up the time taken for the statement to be written, agreed and published. The best position is to have discussed the initial statement within the planning and preparation process that has taken place. The CEO and senior team should have agreed some template statements, which can then be refined to suit the circumstances occurring without the need to gain approval. However, if there is an approval that is needed it should be only one person, who is aware that they must be available to agree the communication immediately.

Wherever possible the first statement should be issued within 20 minutes of the incident or issue emerging, and earlier wherever possible. Communicators should always work to gain the trust of those in charge of the business to benefit them in managing a crisis as it will allow them the freedom to act without requiring approval.

The crisis or situation will develop and at that point more detailed statements and public announcements will be required; this is the stage at which approval becomes essential. Those providing the operational response need to be on hand to ensure that the information being released is accurate and clear. It is at this point that the impact on affected people should also be referenced and the statement focused on the human impact of the crisis. The first statement may include this, but as detailed information will be sketchy do not try to add in information that may be unclear. Ensure that you are focusing on the people affected and imagine them hearing your communication – what would they think? If they are not going to be comfortable with what is said, then you should reconsider the wording and approach that is being used. Crises have a significant impact on people and in many situations there will be a sense of loss and grieving. This makes it even more critical that wording is sensitive, thoughtful and focused on the people at the centre of the crisis.

Crisis situations can be won or lost on the way the affected people are managed, supported and assisted. Affected people can be those involved in the crisis or whose relatives and friends are involved, but they are also the employees of the organization involved in the response. We will cover this more in Chapter 4.

The public statements need to be written, developed and shared quickly, which moves the situation forward in proactively managing the issue or incident. Remember to have a stakeholder engagement plan in your crisis communication plan, which can provide a list of who the statements need to be sent to, with a detailed hierarchy of importance. This is vital because it means you will be starting the conversation rather than trying to join it part-way through when people will have started to make up their own narrative. A clear narrative for all parties, from stakeholders to staff and affected people to the general public, helps people to make sense of what has happened. This narrative can be updated, developed and refined as the crisis develops. This should be made clear from the start of the communication.

Misinformation, disinformation and fake news

Modern communication has been heavily affected by the growth of incorrect news and information or commentary, and things that are not quite what they seem at face value. There are different elements of this that can be in place when a crisis happens: misinformation, disinformation and fake news.

Misinformation refers to inaccurate and false information that is shared regardless of whether it is intended to mislead. This can happen when an incident occurs and people attempt to fill any gaps in knowledge and understanding of the issue. They make assumptions and can use previous experience to try to define what is happening with the current situation. Counteracting it can be through providing as much information as possible and correcting inaccuracies quickly to avoid them spreading.

Disinformation is more problematic as it relates to false information that is deliberately shared with an aim of misleading people. Information that has been shared can be manipulated in an attempt to claim a different narrative from what was intended. Propaganda is a form of disinformation as it is information that is intentionally biased or misleading to promote a particular viewpoint.

Dealing with disinformation is more challenging as merely correcting the inaccuracy will not stop those intent on spreading it. It requires careful thought and an approach that attempts to marginalize the inaccurate viewpoint.

Fake news is totally inaccurate information that is crafted to be misleading, in an attempt to appear as mainstream news. This information is often sensationalized and full of emotion. It is important with fake news to understand what is accurate, what is misinterpreted and what is totally false before deciding on the course of action to take. Alongside this it is important to understand who the source of the fake news is. Is it a mainstream media outlet? Is it a blogger or online influencer? Is it from an activist or campaigner, or a member of the public?

With all three issues it is important to have a clear plan for how they will be approached, what will be done and who has the responsibility for undertaking any actions. This should form part of a crisis communication strategy with a focus on how each problem will be addressed, who will carry out the work and how its impact will be assessed. Never underestimate the potential impact that misinformation, disinformation and fake news can have on developing effective crisis communication.

Who can we learn from?

Dealing with crises is something that a few organizations do on a regular basis. The military and emergency services face a range of crises more frequently than any other organizations. In developing the crisis communication approach and our processes to deal with situations it is worth reviewing how these organizations operate, to identify if there are any transferable aspects. The importance of a structure and framework to both identify risks and manage situations has been highlighted previously. The military and emergency services appear to be more able to manage crisis situations due to the nature of their daily business. They are already structured to work round the clock, which means there will be communication support available 24 hours a day, seven days a week. They are also organizations that invest more in planning and preparing for possible crisis situations. They have relevant plans and they will exercise them regularly. These organizations will also have a strong business continuity and risk management function.

All businesses should recognize that the investment in development, training and exercising of the crisis response will put the business in a state of readiness that will assist in providing an effective coordination of the organizational response. Emergency planning is a critical part of the operation of any organization or business and should not be overlooked.

A military approach

The military around the world are a uniform service with a strong disciplined approach to the work that they do. There are many reasons why they are successful in responding to unexpected situations. When they are faced with challenging situations that require clear decision making under pressure they use their approach to full effect. Six key elements of the approach can be reflected on to assist communicators preparing to plan for and deal with a crisis:

1 Training and learning
2 Right person for the job
3 Clear procedures
4 Hierarchy of decision making
5 Support mechanisms
6 Debriefing

Training and learning

There are very few times that the military will be called on to work at their top level and potentially face the enemy on the battlefield. But this does not stop them continually training to be able to move swiftly from a resting state to a place where they may be called on to face an enemy. This focus on ongoing training and the exercises that are carried out is essential for the military to be able to perform effectively. All the time spent is essential to ensure that they can do the job properly, therefore this time is an investment. It is not seen as wasted effort. As discussed in Chapter 1, this keeps the organization in a state of readiness where learning has happened in a safe environment, allowing plans to be refined, adapted and ready for use.

Right person for the job

People are chosen because of their skills, abilities and experience in key areas. Not all military personnel at the same level will have the same abilities and choosing the right person who can perform the tasks most effectively is a key strength. Each person has a specific role to perform and, as mentioned, will have been testing themselves and their ability to undertake it. Having an awareness of who is best at what will be critical to ensure there is a high-functioning team in place. For communicators it is about using those with a personable nature to undertake the work to support affected people and even staff wellbeing, or it may be about having the media specialists taking a lead on responding to the deluge of questions that will be received during and after a crisis. The military know where the skills are, so they are then able to fit the person to the right role. This is the situation even if the role being carried out differs from the usual activities that are undertaken.

Clear procedures

All organizations will have a range of procedures in place but not all employees will know what exists and how they will work to support those systems. Knowing the details of the plans and processes is a vital part of any well-run business. The military operate within a strict framework of what is acceptable behaviour but also of how they are expected to work. Every business will have procedures that ensure the effective daily running of the operation. But everyone needs to understand them and what they mean, to know what behaviour is acceptable and how they should operate. This is all activity that can be achieved during the preparation phase and before any crisis emerges and needs to be faced. The procedures can be a support mechanism to use.

Hierarchy of decision making

The hierarchical nature of the way the military is structured makes it clear who reports to whom and where the chain of command exists. This sense of strong governance is at the heart of effective crisis response processes. Decisions can be made at each level but there are set parameters of what can be done at what level. It means the front-line can take action and decide certain things, but they are aware of when to refer decision making upwards or to wait for orders from the top. This command and control approach ensures there is no confusion about what has been done and there are no gaps that emerge. It is a way of ensuring the situation is approached with a united front, that all the required elements, activities and decisions are made at the appropriate level, and all the players are aware of what it is and where it is from. Lacking this sort of clear structure can create delays as it must be established from scratch, which in the heat of a crisis can lead to significant problems including loss of confidence and operational failures.

Support mechanisms

Along with the fact that everyone has their clearly defined place, the military also operate alongside other supporting organizations. In many countries they are part of NATO and are a function of the government. It gives them state approval for their activities and actions, which supports the justification of their approach to dealing with the situation. But it also means they have access to additional resources, specialisms, equipment and professionals. This ensures they are unlikely to feel overwhelmed by any situation and they can also tap into expert knowledge from those who may have experienced a similar circumstance. Businesses are always trying to keep costs low and avoid unnecessary spending. This can be a challenge when a crisis hits and when putting time and money into preparations for crisis management.

Debriefing

Testing and exercising are important as part of the development of the appropriate plans but so is the debrief process. After every significant event, manoeuvre or activity there will be a structured approach to reviewing the deployment and what worked, and where improvements could be made. It works from the start of the activity through to the conclusion. It ensures all the decision making is assessed and consideration is given to whether improvements could be made. It creates a learning environment where the experiences of individuals can be assessed and shared. Alongside this is a culture where people want to do their best and no one wants to be found falling short at the most critical moment in their career. This places a lot of personal responsibility on the individual members of each platoon or squad.

Through each of these six elements you can see the focus on the individual as part of a team. It is the team approach that brings the biggest rewards for the military. Structure, skills, processes and support are all built around getting the best from the personnel and ensuring they can work together to achieve the required outcome. Many businesses lack a sufficient focus on the importance of having a high-performing team in place that can achieve results. Just having the right processes will not bring the results you require to ensure staff are actively involved in being prepared. This will be covered further in the next chapter when we look at the people involved in the crisis and consider employee communication and engagement.

The emergency services approach

Emergency services also have some similar approaches to the military that provide key areas of support to manage during a time of crisis. However, emergency services will face more challenges in relation to the support of affected people and managing the long-term impact of the crisis. The police, fire and ambulance services will be the ones offering immediate care and attention to any affected individuals but also will need to continue this throughout the crisis and even into the recovery phase. The focus for emergency services when faced with a crisis is to preserve and protect life first and foremost. This is the thread through all emergency responses. It is worthwhile understanding how the emergency services work during a crisis so that if you are caught up in an incident you know what will be happening and what that means for your business' communication approach. In the UK the Chartered Institute of Public Relations published a document in 2019 providing information on how organizations can manage communication when a terrorist attack happens. All organizations and businesses could find themselves caught up in an emergency services-led crisis, so it should be part of preparations and planning.

There are eight key elements of the emergency services approach:

1 Command and control approach
2 Structural support
3 Exercising
4 Role identified in legislation
5 Managing the consequences
6 Focusing on the human aspects
7 Tactical advisers
8 Debriefing

Command and control approach

In dealing with a disaster or emergency there will be a strict structure in place with a Gold Commander in overall control. The Gold Commander will be a very senior person within the organization and will set the overarching strategy. They will make the most critical decisions related to the response. They are supported by Silver Commanders who have some decision-making responsibility and Bronze Commanders who will be working tactically on the ground. It can be referred to as strategic (Gold), tactical (Silver) and operational (Bronze). Silver Commanders coordinate all the individual plans in place to ensure they are supporting the strategy that has been set. Bronze Commanders are responsible for developing the plans for their operational area of responsibility. Decisions can be taken at each level – Bronze, Silver or Gold – but these are carefully controlled. Those with responsibility for key areas will be expected to undertake the actions required by those above them. Hence it is known as command and control.

Structural support

The Gold, Silver, Bronze approach has a clear structure around it, and this means that at each level they have clear decision-making responsibilities. Commanders will be the ones leading in the key areas of the response, which can include, for example, investigation, intelligence, community issues, communication and welfare. The structure also includes regular briefings and meetings that will assess progress, each area having a plan in place that they are working to. The meetings check on the progress of those plans and whether the situation has changed, requiring an alteration in the course of action.

Exercising

Emergency services organizations have departments established that are staffed with people who are responsible for building emergency plans, reviewing developments that may impact on existing plans, and developing training and exercising of plans. They may be members of the Emergency Planning Society in the UK, or similar organizations in other countries. Such organizations promote the importance of resilience and ensuring preparedness within institutions, organizations and businesses. These departments will involve people as required at all stages of their work. It means there is a continued focus on exercising and ensuring a readiness to deal with a crisis. This includes a programme of work on exercises that takes place throughout the year, something that may appear excessive for many businesses but is a defendable position for those charged with being the first responders in an emergency.

Role identified in legislation

The position for emergency services organizations is that they have a requirement to undertake actions during a crisis. In the UK there is a Civil Contingencies Act that establishes the role for emergency services. In the USA there are Acts of Congress that outline the position. The actions and responsibilities are laid down in legislation that charges them with the role as first responders. This means they can face severe penalties if they are not ready and able to perform these functions immediately. If there are inquiries and reviews that find they were ill prepared for any reason, then ultimately it can mean some form of sanction being put in place.

Managing the consequences

Unlike the military response, the police and law enforcement agencies have to take a long-term view of managing a crisis. This can be over many years, particularly if the police have to carry out a lengthy investigation, for example. They have a responsibility for community cohesion and ensuring that there is a return to normality within society. This requires a strand of work during any crisis that looks at the impact the event or issue has had on key communities, individuals or organizations. It combines stakeholder mapping with the operational response and the communication activity. Communication is an essential part of what is known as consequence management as it ensures there is a consistent narrative across all forms of communication including face-to-face conversations that are not within the corporate communications remit. It can prevent confusion or concern among communities but also alert the responders to emerging issues that may impact on their work. We will explore this further in Chapter 6 looking at the community.

Focusing on the human aspects

Supporting victims and their families and those affected by a crisis is within the responsibility of the police with support from other public sector organizations and third sector charity agencies. Emergencies will require family liaison officers being assigned to those affected. These are usually police employees who are there to provide information to support people through the incident and the events that follow. This will include support when faced with things such as inquests and inquiries. The impact on people will be considered from an early stage within the police structured meeting process, with a coordinator or senior officer providing information and updates. At the heart of this is an attempt to keep those involved and affected updated during a fast-moving crisis so that they are not damaged or further affected by learning about developments second- or third-hand. Again, this will be discussed further in Chapter 6.

Tactical advisers

The emergency services response must cover many areas of responsibility as previously outlined within the discussion on the structured approach. To support this, those with areas of expertise are given the responsibility of being tactical advisers. The advisers will be expected to provide details of the best possible course of action to take, to understand the detail of the processes and guidance, and to be working at the top of their area of expertise. While they are often quite junior officers in terms of rank, they will have developed their expertise to a point that makes them the 'go-to person' within the organization. This advice will then be provided to the officer in charge to help inform their decision making during the incident. The key is that people are recognized for their expertise and encouraged to take on the adviser roles. Commanders at senior levels need to be open to listen and act on their guidance and advice. Communication at this point must also be able to operate at both strategic and tactical levels. It is why the structured response should identify the roles and responsibilities, ensuring that there is a clear strategic lead for communication but also that the tactical roles are in place to deliver the plan.

Debriefing

In a similar way to the military, law enforcement will be focused on ensuring debriefs take place looking at all areas of the response, and considering what worked and what could be improved for the future. Unlike in the military, these reviews will often involve other agencies that have also been involved in the response and will happen both immediately after the main incident – which is known as a 'hot debrief' – and in the longer term to ensure the recovery phase is also subject to review. The UK College of Policing has set down a structured debrief process where all aspects of the police response will be reviewed and if needed trained staff can be brought in to assist the process. At the end there will be a detailed document that will include a plan to address any issues of concern that were raised. The communication approach will be part of the structured debrief but the communication team can also consider discussions with communicators from other agencies or the media to assess the communication strategy and plan and how the implementation of it worked. It is important when running debriefs to stress the reasons why they are undertaken. Debriefs are not about apportioning blame but should be about improving the response, identifying urgent actions and building for a stronger recovery. When undertaking debriefs this point needs to be stressed so people are open and comfortable sharing both what worked and what needs to be improved.

The emergency services structure benefits communication because they have a seat as tactical adviser to assist in the development of the response. However, alongside this there is a significant amount of pressure from supporting affected people, getting the right messages out and being subject to intense scrutiny. This will be considered in Chapter 7. However, the fact there is a chance to get communication within the crisis plans and to be able to test them puts emergency services communicators at an advantage when something happens.

Other approaches

There are other structures and approaches to crisis management that may bring additional benefits and challenges to the communicator. In some situations it may be more effective to have a collaborative approach rather than a response controlled by a single agency. This will require significant agreements about working arrangements and a mature approach to the way management operates. In this response all agencies will stand and work together, sharing ideas and suggestions for how to move forward. It supports the coherent narrative and will avoid organizations moving to a negative blame scenario focused on others. But it can lead to inaction and inertia if there is too much discussion and negotiation taking place that prevents action.

A legal response is often seen to be the most beneficial to a business. There will be concern about legal action emerging from the incident or issue and the legal team will be aware of the potential problems they may face. Legal challenges are costly to the business and damaging to the reputation so the CEO managing a crisis may put more weight on the advice from the legal team than from the communication function. This leads to the traditional problem of legal advice being contrary to communication advice, which creates problems for those leading the response to the crisis. What communicators can provide to this situation that the legal team will not be able to is a clear understanding of the emotions of the situation and the human toll of what has taken place. With the relevant data, insight and information to support this, they can then start to leverage a place at the top table and the ear of those in charge of managing the crisis, so that they are a tactical adviser in the same way as the head of legal and occupy the same space. In the same way that lawyers will use case law as an evidence base for their advice, so communicators should be comfortable using case studies of crisis communication activity to provide evidence to support their advice. Doing what is right from a legal standpoint will not always match the right course of action from a communication perspective. The ability to influence those in charge is an essential skill for the communicator not just during a crisis but for 365 days a year.

Finally, you have the potential business-focused approach to the crisis, which can often be clearly aligned to a legal approach. The central tenet of the response will be to do what supports the business, and the structure will potentially involve shareholders and key stakeholders. It is the share price and the potential impact on the stock exchange that will be the priority and the support will be gathered around that. This is a potentially flawed approach if it is the main aim of the crisis response as it can forget the human impact of the incident. In the eyes of the public, who will be looking at the impact on people, this will not be an acceptable approach and can have the reverse effect of what it attempts to achieve. Rather than securing the business it can put things on shaky ground. A better position is to have a tactical adviser who will monitor the impact of the crisis on stocks and shares and provide guidance on how this can be managed. This can then be assessed alongside community issues, legal advice and communication guidance.

A strong framework

From all the operational approaches we have considered there are seven aspects that need to be in place for the business to have a strong framework for crisis management:

1 **Ensure that the business appoints people to lead**
   These are people with clear areas of responsibility with each led by a named individual. This covers the demand for specialist guidance and advice together with a clear decision-making process. It mirrors the crisis communication strategy in having clear roles with key actions assigned to each.

2 **Bring everyone together in one room, whether virtually or in person**
   If you can bring together the key commanders or leaders who have areas of responsibility, even if this is for the first few hours

of a crisis emerging, then you will have a more consistent and coherent response. It allows people to operate with speed while consulting with key decision-makers and take agreed decisive action to support the over-arching business strategy to manage the crisis. Having a 'war room' where people can come together and work to bring things under control is hugely beneficial.

3   **Planning and testing keep people in a state of readiness**
This should always be remembered. We have seen from the work of the military, law enforcement and the emergency services that planning and preparing are critical elements to support operational success in managing any crisis. It ensures structures, systems and processes are in place and assessed for effectiveness, and that employees are trained and understand what is required of them. They can then be ready for action.

4   **Have the right person in the right role**
If you have a clear plan, then you need the right trained and skilled people to lead in key areas. The military will use the right people for the right role and in all organizations that is going to be important. Use people's skills and experience in the right way and put them where they will be able to do their best. This creates the culture where they will want to succeed and show how they can support the team response.

5   **Understand the implications and those affected so you can manage the consequences**
Identifying the impact of the crisis, whether it is an operational or reputational issue, will provide support through the initial management and right through to the recovery phase. It requires using the understanding of events, as well as data about customers and service users, and other insight to see the incident or event's touchpoints. Having conducted some scenario planning you will be able to utilize this to map the groups and individuals likely to be affected.

6   **Keep communication integrated**
Bring all the communication together so that there is a consistent narrative regardless of the channel and the audience. Everything

that is provided helps people to make sense of what has happened and to understand the course of events. This does not mean hiding or withholding key information; rather, it is about providing the context that is required to assist the response phase. Make sure the response puts systems in place to update employees and stakeholders behind the scenes, as well as the victims, victims' families and affected people, with similar information, to minimize the risk of anyone learning about what has happened from an unofficial source, or second-hand.

7 **Focus on the human cost and doing what is right, not what is going to protect the reputation of the business**
If decisions are made purely to protect the reputation of the organization or to ensure there is limited impact on the share price, then they will be potentially flawed. The decision making will be based upon a small section of information and, as we will see in many of the case studies throughout the book, failing to consider the human cost of the situation will threaten the success of any crisis communication activity. The reputation of the business should be built upon the actions that are taken and not just in communication alone.

Communication at the heart of the response

Businesses may see the critical aspects of the response as being focused on developing the operational activity to tackle what has happened or to move things forward. The operational activity is central and does have to be in place for communication to be effective. But the communication must sit alongside this operational activity and be equally important. The two parts must go hand in hand for the most effective response. Without clear, consistent and focused communication, all the operational activity will take place without public recognition and the perception of the business will not be managed.

Communication can address several key issues that impact on or derail the operational response. It is where the operational benefits from the crisis communication strategy and plan that have been developed can be seen. First, the communication function must have a seat in the 'war room'. They need to be at the heart of the operational developments so that they can advise at an early stage and get the latest situational updates to inform the communication plan. As things will be potentially fast moving then, the communicator must be able to get instant updates so that they fully understand the unfolding situation.

Having a clear narrative, as we have mentioned, ensures the organization can address what has happened and start to take people on a journey to reach the recovery phase. The benefit is that the consistency builds trust and confidence in the response as employees, stakeholders, affected people and the wider community will all hear the same information. In the early stages of the crisis the communicator should be gathering all the known information and details of where the gaps in knowledge are, to start to be able to develop the wording that is required. This narrative will be updated and developed as more information becomes available and the crisis develops. It is essential to ensure that all the required people have access to the latest statement or narrative for consistency, so systems need to be in place for the quick dissemination of information across the business.

The communicator must also work closely with the spokesperson, who should in many cases be the chief executive or person at the very top of the business or organization. The CEO will have to step up and show leadership throughout the crisis and hitting the right note with the communication content and delivery is essential. The tactics, approach and activity all need to be informed by the advice and guidance from the communication lead. It requires positive working relationships to be in place before any crisis emerges so that there is trust and confidence when the pressure is on. The role of the CEO and other key leaders will be considered in more detail in Chapter 5.

In the modern era with the developments in social media, a crisis is likely to be beset by the problem of 'fake news'. This can be deliberately created to impact on the response to the incident or issue, or it may be inaccurate but without malice. Dealing with the two aspects can require slightly different courses of action. In the first instance where inaccurate statements are made, they should be immediately challenged. This is why having a media and social media monitoring team working from the start of the crisis is so critical. If the communication team is operating at the heart of the operational response, they will know what is accurate and what is inaccurate, accepting there may be a grey area in the middle. They must then have the freedom to be able to quickly and robustly challenge statements that are wrong or inaccurate. It may mean complaining to social media platform operators or making a complaint to the media outlet or the regulatory bodies should the initial approach be unsuccessful. If no action is taken to remove or retract the inaccuracy, then the organization should consider going proactive to discredit the inaccurate news and provide an honest account to clarify the position. This needs to be included in the crisis communication plan to ensure that it is part of the consistent response and to identify opportunities where challenge can be made.

Some business leaders may wonder what the point is of challenging inaccurate or fake information if media outlets, social media platform operators and regulatory bodies are not going to remove or correct the information. However, in the recovery phase when the actions of the organization may be scrutinized or brought into question, they need to be seen to have attempted to take action to deal with inaccuracies. Failure to do so makes it appears as though the business is complicit with the publication of the information.

If the information is inaccurate but without malice, then a starting point is to attempt to develop a conversation with the publisher with a view to them making a correction. Speed of the response in doing this is essential to try to prevent it becoming widely published or shared. If you can start that conversation early and the publisher agrees to correct the information, then you can deal with it and move forward.

The communication team can also utilize the information and knowledge that they have to operate as a representative for those who are affected by the crisis. They can provide a voice within the operational response that asks, 'How will those affected view this activity?' In developing the communication response, it is advantageous to have the affected individuals supportive of the approach and the content of the communication. If you are not able to achieve this, then you should at least ensure that the individuals receive the details before they are made public. Communication activity must be sensitive to the impact that the issue or incident has had, and this is where the consequence management needs to be in place. Ensure that you consider the concerns of people, groups and communities. This will be covered in more detail in Chapter 6.

Finally, the communication team must start to bring all the elements together so that they can begin the task of preparing the plan not only for dealing with the current crisis but for considering the move to recovery and the long-term plans for the organization. As soon as practicable the plan for the crisis being faced should be documented, together with those long-term considerations that will need to be revisited as the crisis develops.

CASE STUDY
Pepsi advert and Oxfam crisis

In 2017, drinks company Pepsi launched an advertising campaign that sparked outrage. It came off the back of protests in the United States linked to the Black Lives Matter movement and appeared to mirror imagery from those protests. The advert featured model and reality star Kendall Jenner appearing to quash a disturbance between police and protests by opening a can of the drink. The response was almost immediate and within a short time Pepsi had removed the advert from social media, although it was continuing to be shared.[1]

A senior executive apologized and issued a statement that said: 'Clearly we missed the mark, and we apologize. We did not intend to make light of any serious issue. We are removing the content and halting any further rollout.'[2]

This shows that it was taking swift action to deal with the offence that may have been caused by the advert. It also ensured that the action came from someone in a very senior position. There was no intention to blame others, which again added to the accountability and responsibility being taken by the brand. It continued to apologize also to Kendall Jenner, which showed some attention to those impacted by the crisis. However, to build on this, Pepsi could have spoken to some of the key groups affected and looked at addressing the diversity issues of its management and brand development to rebuild confidence. The role of the communicator working alongside the senior executives to frame the response and the development is critical in reputational crises. This allows the long-term recovery to be prepared and considered during the initial response.

If we compare the response from Pepsi with a different reputational issue that affected the charity Oxfam, we see the importance of being swift and decisive. In 2018 it faced 10 days of reporting about the sensitive issue that it had hushed up claims of sexual exploitation by aid workers in Haiti, and there were also reports of sexual harassment by workers in its shops. Charities require public confidence to ensure people continue to support with finances and bring in government funding. The response to these concerns was criticized for being slow and focusing initially on the fact it had followed their processes in dealing with the allegations. However, this also put the spotlight on its decision to deal with the matters in this way, appearing to avoid any public scrutiny.[3]

The focus on the process when dealing with such a sensitive and emotive issue added to negative commentary, which then impacted its reputation. This was always going to be a challenging situation to face but the response was seen to 'have an air of inconvenience' to the management.[4]

In addition to the concerns about the focus of the initial response, it was also slow to react to the criticism and to put a senior executive in front of the media. It reminds us of the importance of effective media training for all those who are in executive levels within organizations and particularly to undertake this with a focus on a crisis response for those who will be taking that responsibility. In this digital world it still remains a fundamental skill for any senior manager to be able to effectively handle a media interview.[5]

At the heart of this situation Oxfam seemed to lack openness and transparency, which are critical for voluntary and charity organizations that rely on public and government donations. The approach appeared defensive and did not appear to recognize the need to make changes to the systems and processes that it had in place. It then did not seem to recognize the need to make changes to the way it worked so the same situation could not happen again.[6]

It has been estimated by a brand valuation report analysed by *PR Week* that £400 million was wiped from the value of the Oxfam brand due to the issue and how it was handled.[7] If we look at both cases it is clear there needs to be a structured approach to the crisis where communication can operate at the heart of the response. Building in the consequence management and voice of those affected would have assisted the response to both issues and, in the case of Pepsi, had there been an external overview the crisis may never have occurred as the advert would never have been made or broadcast.

Being in a state of readiness will support making a swift and decisive response that has taken account of all the factors identified as important to the organization. Emergency procedures should take us into that structured response, supporting both operational and communication activity.

Both cases also emphasize the importance of the wording used in the first statement and the feeling that it conveys. In the case of Pepsi it was recognized as being decisive but for Oxfam was seen to be dismissive of the situation.[8]

Key learning points

- Honesty and openness are always fundamental to all forms of communication to manage a crisis or critical situation.

- Ensure that the structured response to crises has provided training and support to those who will be leading areas of work. This should include media and communication training to help those at the top of the organization to understand not only the actions that are required from them but the way in which communication should be delivered.

- Put communication within the crisis response team so that the strategic communication lead can provide advice and guidance to the team developing the response. Allow communicators to provide case studies, consultation information, data and insight to assist in understanding the implications both of the crisis and of the consequences of the response.

- Bring diverse voices into your crisis communication. This will be covered in Chapter 6 looking at building diversity and inclusion into your communication response. Consultation can assist the team in viewing the situation from the perspective of others, which is vital to developing effective crisis communication.

- Never appear dismissive in the response to a crisis. Whether it is seen as a critical situation for the business or not is irrelevant. If people are concerned about what has happened and it has damaged the trust and confidence they have in the organization or business then it must be taken seriously. Explaining what has happened should be done clearly and honestly but not dismissively.

Conclusion

Remaining calm during a crisis is important. It will allow you to keep a clear head to develop the right approach and to make the right decisions. More than all that it means you will remember that the plan exists and what it means. You can take a deep breath and then use the preparation work to ensure you act quickly to address the crisis response.

A crisis can come from anywhere and from any set of circumstances. Inevitably, it will probably emerge from where you least expect it and from what you have invested little time in planning for. All that should not matter if the strategy you have developed can be reviewed and refined to meet any eventuality. Don't get too focused on trying to identify all the risks and situations that could become a crisis. Instead, ensure that you have an approach that gives you the foundations to build a bespoke and effective communication response and the flexibility to adjust depending on the circumstances that are being faced.

Understand the process that is in place within the business to declare that a crisis is occurring. Be clear about what that means for the communication function and what is required from the communicators. If this isn't clear, then work to develop that element of the response. In some cases the business does not have a clear escalation procedure to raise emerging issues that may become a crisis; if you find this, then make senior leaders aware it is not in place and that it is a requirement for an effective crisis management plan. Use your communication skills, knowledge and experience to help the business develop an escalation process.

Tailor your crisis communication strategy into a plan that will meet the circumstances of the crisis you face. Treat it as a unique situation and consider what those circumstances mean for the way you approach the communication activity. This includes ensuring you consider the impact on all affected groups, which must include employees.

Remember that you don't have to deal with the incident alone. Look at how other organizations structure and prepare for a crisis, especially those such as the military and emergency services, which deal with them regularly. Identify what, from their structure and approach, may work within your crisis communication response. Call for help if you need it, from colleagues, experts or others.

Notes

1 D Victor. Pepsi pulls ad accused of trivializing Black Lives Matter, *New York Times*, 5 April 2017. www.nytimes.com/2017/04/05/business/kendall-jenner-pepsi-ad.amp.html (archived at perma.cc/JK6C-UUH3)

2 D Quenqua. Pepsi says 'sorry' and removes Kendall Jenner ad from the web, *PR Week*, 5 April 2017. www.prweek.com/article/1429761/pepsi-says-sorry-removes-kendall-jenner-ad-web (archived at perma.cc/DE2U-CET4)

3 Oxfam International. Oxfam's reaction to sexual misconduct story in Haiti, 9 February 2018. www.oxfam.org/en/pressroom/reactions/oxfams-reaction-sexual-misconduct-story-haiti (archived at perma.cc/7YEA-E9P9)

4 L Weymouth. Oxfam: We 'failed to get the tone right' in initial responses to Haiti scandal, *Charity Times*, 4 July 2018. www.charitytimes.com/ct/oxfam-tone-haiti-scandal.php (archived at perma.cc/R9SQ-ZJMY)

5 BBC Newsnight. Former Oxfam boss knew of sexual misconduct claims (online video), 12 February 2018. www.youtube.com/watch?v=VwlH0XtmA3Y (archived at perma.cc/S2C3-TVS4)

6 BBC News (UK). 'We didn't hide this' – Dame Barbara Stocking, former Oxfam chief executive, on how charity reacted to allegations that some of its aid workers in Haiti used prostitutes [Twitter] 9 February 2018. https://twitter.com/bbcnews/status/961973341023191041?lang=en (archived at perma.cc/5HJK-9W2V)

7 A Hickman. Oxfam sex scandal wiped £400m from brand valuation, report reveals, *PR Week*, 9 January 2019. www.prweek.com/article/1522440/oxfam-sex-scandal-wiped-400m-brand-valuation-report-reveals (archived at perma.cc/9FKJ-5KG3)

8 Z Bangura and K Sierra. Committing to Change, Protecting People: Toward a more accountable Oxfam. Final Report. Independent Commission on Sexual Misconduct, Accountability & Culture Change, June 2019. www-cdn.oxfam.org/s3fs-public/oxfam_ic_final_report-en.pdf (archived at perma.cc/67H9-EBDG)

4

Remembering the people: How employees should come first

All the processes and procedures will be of no benefit if they fail to take account of the human cost of the impact of the crisis. Remembering the people involved and those affected, and using this to improve your actions, means a greater possibility of developing an effective crisis communication response.

Up to this point in the book we have talked a lot about the external audiences and the people outside the organization. This has included ensuring that there is a swift response to manage potential public criticism, which will emerge quickly. During a crisis, that is what communicators often do – they focus exclusively on the external communication activity at the expense of considering the staff, employees and stakeholders. The Covid-19 pandemic did go some way to changing this approach, as employee communication became essential to how businesses functioned through restrictions and the requirements to work from home. There is nothing more important than developing a crisis communication response that has people at the heart of it.

If you have planned and prepared appropriately then you will have a detailed understanding of your external and internal audiences that can be utilized during a crisis. More than that, you will have found ways to involve people in the planning, testing and exercising of the response. The external audience can include all the groups mentioned in Chapter 1 in planning and stakeholder mapping, and Chapter 3 where we considered consequence management. The key to consequence management is understanding what is happening and being able to assess and consider what may follow. This then allows the communicator to use their knowledge and experience of targeting audiences to identify who the affected parties are likely to be. The plan can then ensure that they are reached with communication actions. The same approach would be beneficial in considering the internal audience. Start by looking at those who may be involved, the wider teams who are affected because of the nature of the issue or incident and the rest of the employees who will be continuing to make the business run during the crisis. This will be covered in more detail later in this chapter.

Involving people

First, you need to consider whether you are going to be active or passive in communicating and connecting with your key audiences. This is the same consideration for both external and internal audiences. Passive engagement will often happen in the early stages of a crisis when communicators are looking to broadcast messages to key groups. As we have already mentioned this is a very short initial phase in the lifetime of the crisis. It is focused on giving people direct information to ensure they are safe and protected. The plan should look to move to communication that is engaging as quickly as possible as the crisis develops. The same may be said for the communication to employees within the business. In the initial stages it is likely to be information that is broadcast for them either to act on or to share appropriately but it must move to engagement quickly as they will then be able to more effectively support the crisis response.

Active engagement is the desired state of crisis communication. It is where communication should be once the first wave of the crisis has emerged and subsided. Once implemented it will allow thinking time, the chance to develop activity and a two-way flow of information creating an ongoing conversation. This is when time should be taken to consider how to involve key groups and individuals in the communication response. There are many ways to involve people. They could be brought in to see the response and understand the actions that the organization is taking. For example, in the case of a product failure key individuals from the shareholders, the consumers and community representatives could be brought into the plant room, design suite or other key locations to see the work under way. Bringing people into the heart of the response is a way to build confidence in the response. Another possibility is to go and talk to key groups and individuals. For example, if you are a small business that has undertaken building work that has negatively impacted the surrounding neighbours, one of the best ways to involve people is to go and meet residents to discuss the situation.

Making connections

Developing relationships is at the core of all effective communication and during a crisis this doesn't change. Dealing with an incident is a time when your hard work in creating connections through communication throughout the year should bring you benefits. If the relationships are strong then you will be able to quickly get in touch with the right individuals and start to share information, and work to bring them into discussions about the communication response. But this all needs to be part of your daily work. There is no way you can develop effective relationships quickly when you are under pressure dealing with a crisis. As outlined in Chapter 1, invest time when you are not in crisis to equip you to respond to an incident when it happens. This includes ensuring that your communication activity considers a number of additional areas, including community engagement, consequence management and employee engagement.

In Chapter 6 we will consider community engagement in more detail when we look at community and consequence management. We will also consider how you can involve people in reviewing and adapting the narrative and communication approach based on their knowledge and experience.

The internal audience

The operational response to the crisis is only possible with the hard work, commitment and dedication of the employees of the business. If they are involved and engaged, they will ensure there is an effective response because they take responsibility for it. Employees are the most important part of any business. It is why we should keep staff at the forefront of our communication activity when we are dealing with a crisis. Systems and process are important to managing the response but the biggest factor contributing to the success will be the people involved. Employees have a key role in all the phases of the crisis response from planning through to recovery. They should have the freedom to provide feedback on the actions being proposed throughout the response.

Employee engagement is what effective companies are built upon. The staff feel a deep connection to the business and want to do their best to ensure success. This is reciprocated with an organization that involves and listens to them, valuing their contribution and their wellbeing. Opening the floor to staff suggestions may appear to be a contradiction to having a very structured response to a crisis. This is not the case and misunderstands how organizations can and should operate. The structure is required so that people know their area of responsibility and the level of decision making that they can be involved in. It gives clarity about what they should do and how it fits together. However, this does not mean that people cannot provide their valuable insight and input into managing the situation. It is essential if the response is to be as effective as possible. There is a close relationship with employee engagement and wellbeing, which we consider in more detail in Chapter 7.

Learning the language

In the planning phase that we outlined in Chapter 1 the full involvement of employees is essential. They must assist in the development of the structures, plans and processes that support crisis management. In ensuring involvement it supports the creation of a state of readiness across the business. People will understand what is expected of them and the role they play in managing the response or keeping the business running while the crisis is underway. Staff need to have been involved in testing and exercising the response, so they understand the language of crisis. Imagine learning a new language; you need to take time to see how the words fit together to make sentences and then how those sentences can make a conversation. This is the same for staff who need to understand the approach, what they should do and how it fits together. You cannot expect the employees to be fluent in the language the moment a crisis emerges, so take time to develop their abilities in the planning stages.

The debriefing of these exercises will give people actions to undertake that will revise and improve the plans and move the organization towards a better state of preparedness. It is also an opportunity to reinforce the approach detailed in the crisis communication strategy. The involvement needs to continue throughout the crisis management process, but the critical phase is in the planning and preparation. All staff should also be involved and aware of the risk management processes that exist within the business. They will be able to act as an early warning system highlighting possible issues or areas of concern and should be encouraged to raise them so that they can be considered. This will allow mitigation to be developed to minimize the chance of a situation they have highlighted becoming a crisis.

Do not underestimate how much benefit there is in investing in the workforce and their knowledge, understanding and experience of preparing for any form of crisis. When a crisis happens, they will need to be ready to respond. It is no good having managers ready to deal with the situation that emerges if the frontline employees are unclear what to do, where to go for updates, how to gather information and what is expected of them. For the most seamless and effective response, the organization from top to bottom must be ready, prepared and resilient to deal with the task ahead.

Careless words

In the initial stages of a crisis the actions and behaviour of the employees in dealing with the situation and talking about it will directly impact on the trust and confidence felt towards the business. All staff should understand the details of what has happened and what the organization is doing to deal with the issue. They should also be clear about the narrative and know how to deal with questions, queries or comments that are made to them. A careless word or comment could easily derail the communication plan and lead to a loss of confidence. For example, if you are a small business manufacturing a product and an employee is injured at work, imagine the damage caused by one of the team posting about the incident on social media. They may not have the accurate information, and relatives or friends of the injured person may find out through social media. The same can happen if you are a business creating a new system or product that an employee talks about negatively on social media. The views have the potential to impact negatively on the organization and the development of the new element.

Consider all the touchpoints into the organization from customers, consumers or service users and ensure that the staff working in these areas at the time a crisis emerges are given a detailed briefing on what to say. You may want to make that a section in the plan or it could have its own checklist, where you chart the customer-facing roles that demand quick updates, and lines to take when they are being questioned. In this early stage they can calm concerns with well-chosen, comprehensive and open updates to customers or service users. Getting things right with employees in the early stages will create a firm foundation to build upon as the situation develops through to conclusion.

Ensure the crisis communication plan identifies the best ways to alert all staff to the fact a crisis has happened, whether this is via email, internal messaging system or using other technology such as WhatsApp. It depends on what systems you use daily. Don't invent a new system just for crises; instead use what you already have in place. Awareness is the priority that will help to build employees' confidence in the way the business is dealing with the incident or issue.

Once the crisis is underway staff can play their part to demonstrate strength in dealing with the situation. They will know what to say and where to say it. They will be able to share the organizational narrative and assist the communication activity. If they have already been made aware of the situation and the organizational narrative surrounding it, then they are unlikely to unwittingly undermine the approach being taken. Remember the importance of breaking down the employees into key groups and individuals so that you can tailor the information that is provided, ensuring more detail goes where it is needed.

Employees often use social media extensively in a personal capacity and this will continue during a crisis. There may also be staff who are given authorization to post and update the organization's social media in an official capacity. With this latter group you must ensure they are a key group in your internal communication plan and that they receive updates swiftly, first and in as much detail as possible. For those employees who are using social media personally, there should already be a policy in place for whether they can talk in detail about their work and if so, what might be acceptable. Personal use of social media could be part of the employees' contract and also the standards of behaviour that are expected. New staff should be made aware of the boundaries required on social media and education ensures that all are able to use social media personally without concern about any impact on their employment. This work will build a culture in the organization of appropriate social media use, which will be beneficial when dealing with a crisis. Knowledge and experience will already be in place and all that will be required are gentle reminders about appropriate behaviour. Beyond that ensure you recognize the position of the information that you are circulating to the employees. Can it be shared? Do you need to advise them of how they should use social media during the crisis? It is important to provide guidance and advice so that employees don't stray into discussing issues that should be off limits. This must be updated and shared as the crisis unfolds because the guidance to them will need to be adjusted to take account of the developments that take place. But be clear that anything that is said to staff is likely to become public at some point.

Employees and recovery

Finally, employees will play a critical role in the recovery of the organization. They need to be involved in the debriefs and reviews of the actions that were taken and encouraged to provide open and honest feedback to support the change that will be made. Even when a crisis has been effectively managed there is always learning from the experiences and this needs to be gathered and implemented. In doing this the organization will improve and develop, for both the daily business and in the event of a further issue or incident emerging. Debriefs must look at operational activity, people issues such as well-being, communication and engagement with staff, and resourcing. In taking the learning forward there will inevitably be an impact on employees who will need to accept changes to processes, plans and procedures within the business. Working with employees to implement the developments will increase the likelihood of success in embedding new systems and behaviours. Change communication should assist in putting these new processes in place. The road to recovery is one of the most critical areas in dealing with a crisis but often it is the stage that is overlooked. We will look at recovery in more detail in Chapter 8.

Building success in employee engagement

There are four key areas that need to be in place to ensure effective employee engagement during a crisis:

1 Structures
2 Leadership
3 Channels
4 Messages

All these, as we will see, need to be clearly detailed within the crisis plan both for the operational aspects and the crisis communication strategy. It may be beneficial to have a specific internal crisis communication plan that outlines the details of what will happen within the organization when a crisis occurs. It can provide detail of who is doing what, and when, and how it will be assessed to support the broader crisis communication strategy. When developing both plans, care and attention should be paid to ensuring employee engagement is part of the crisis response. Underpinning the four areas is a drive to move from broadcasting messages in internal communication activities to developing a two-way conversation with employees that is based on listening to them.

Listening is one of the most important skills any communicator or business leader can have within their repertoire. It ensures the business can learn and develop. It means the leadership are supportive of a culture of learning and support. This brings new ideas into the workplace and refines activities based on frontline facts. It identifies issues and potential problems at an early stage when employees raise them. In short, listening is fundamental to the development and survival of the business. This is true not only in day-to-day working but critically when a crisis emerges and threatens the future of the business.

Structures

Communicating with employees must be detailed within the crisis communication plan that has been developed. It should be clearly identified within the operational structure as well, so that areas such as HR or personnel and wellbeing can also be developed alongside communication activity. The structure requires a lead for employee engagement based at the centre of the business with a connection into the control room running the crisis. This could be the head of HR or another senior manager. There should also be local leaders who will provide support across the business. This network is critical for all organizations, particularly those that may have locations worldwide. The central communication approach cannot be effective without points of contact within divisions or departments who can connect the leaders with the frontline staff and can feed back issues that are raised. To achieve the required results with the employees there needs to be delegated responsibility for those in leadership and management roles, or others, to undertake communication activity.

Whoever is leading the communication to staff from the centre of the organization needs to be sitting alongside the communication team or, preferably, will be part of that team. They will also be working closely with HR and the wellbeing lead as well as any trade unions or staff associations that exist. In some organizations that are heavily unionized this may be challenging, but the wellbeing and welfare of employees is important for both unions and the business leaders, so that should be a good starting place for discussions to develop from a point of agreement. All these sections can help each other and need to align their activities to ensure a consistent response that will build confidence within employees.

TOP TIP

In your crisis communication plan, detail the role of the internal communication lead. Ensure it includes how decisions will be made and the key reporting lines that exist to authorize actions and information that will be shared. The internal communication needs to be networked across the business and the crisis response. Detail how you will use your network to support the crisis communication response.

Leadership

In Chapter 5 we will look in detail at the role of the leader in managing the crisis, but it is also critical to staff engagement. The leader's role is usually heavily focused on the external communication and being the visible face of the organization to provide reassurance and confidence during and after the crisis, and to support the management of stakeholder relationships. The CEO also has a duty of care, which means considering the welfare and wellbeing of all the employees and this includes being visible and accessible throughout the incident. It requires an investment of time and resources but as outlined this aspect of the crisis communication response is critical to the success of the plan. Having a senior HR manager or member of the executive team to be the person driving the engagement and wellbeing elements of the operational plan will mean things get done. It will ensure that there is a continued focus on the employees and what they need to support them. This will enable there to be a voice at the key decision-making meetings. A leader who remembers all the employees when the organization is under pressure will be rewarded with support from the staff.

Alongside the executive leadership (those at the top of the organization) each division and department within the organization needs to have someone who takes responsibility to work with the lead to share information and provide feedback. This structure may already exist and be used to cascade information around the organization. However, if the structure is not in place, it is important to have identified it in the plan and to equip, train and support those who will be drafted into the internal communication effort. Leaders must place significant importance on this preparatory work to ensure it is not overshadowed by demands from the public, stakeholders and shareholders.

Channels

There are many ways that you can ensure messages are sent and received around the organization during a crisis. Communication teams should already have an internal communication or employee engagement plan in place. This will provide details of how messages are sent around the business, what channels are used, roles and responsibilities, and the evaluation of awareness, engagement and understanding. All the details can inform the internal communication section of the crisis communication plan and the response that is put in place. It is unacceptable to attempt to devise and establish channels of communication while a crisis is underway. You need to go where people expect information to be shared and these channels can include some of the below:

- face-to-face conversations
- briefings either in person or virtually

- visits by senior leaders
- internal social network systems
- organization's intranet
- video messages
- e-newsletters and internal publications

The central consideration must be how much is shared through face-to-face communication and how much is given remotely through systems such as newsletters or the intranet. The decision on what to share and through what channel will be dependent on the culture and operating procedures of the business. If you are a business that runs internationally with staff based at locations worldwide then you will need to conduct much of the activity using technology. However, you would also need to build in ways that the managers and leaders we mentioned earlier will be able to undertake direct communication with their teams. In a smaller business you could invest more time in face-to-face communication. Effective communication cannot rely on one channel or approach unless it is a highly structured workforce that gathers all its information from one repository.

Within the crisis communication plan, you should identify the key channels and when they will be used. In the early stages of a crisis when broadcasting information is going to be the only possible approach, you may use direct email, internal social networks and the intranet to share the key statements and messages. As the situation develops then other activities including face-to-face briefings and visits by senior managers to key locations can be introduced. This is part of the work required to map the approach and response ahead of any issue or incident emerging.

In devising this plan ensure your employees have been segmented so that you can ensure the right people are being reached by the right information. This is something that is undertaken for external communication activity but is rarely considered when working on internal communication. However, mapping key audiences across communication is essential and is the way to undertake consequence management internally. In addition to having segmented the internal

TABLE 4.1   Example of employee communication and engagement chart

Channel	Example	Benefit	Issues	Engagement level
Central communication issued	• Memo • Intranet story • Email	• Speed • Scalability	• Lack of access to IT • Can be ignored	Low
Noticeboard	• Poster • Intranet	• Scalability • Proximity	• Can be ignored • Slow to update	Low
Manager brief	• Cascade briefing process • Team meeting	• Personal • Allows for questions • Trusted source	• Open to interpretation • Depends on manager's approach • Requires time	Moderate
Social discussion	• Blog • Internal social media platform • Intranet discussion forum	• Allows discussion • Different viewpoints • Involves staff	• Lack of central control • Challenges corporate position	High

audience, which may be done on job role, department, geographic location or another key factor, when a crisis happens we need to understand who is the most affected.

A crisis is like a pebble dropping into water. The pebble creates many ripples across the water in the same way that a crisis will affect some staff and departments more severely than others. If you have undertaken some scenario development and testing this will assist you in understanding where the ripples may flow. Develop the internal communication plan with the knowledge of the situation and possible future issues that may emerge. Use the knowledge to outline a staff engagement plan focusing on the specifics of the issue or incident. The success of the employee engagement during the crisis will be linked to having taken time to consider the activity required in detail and ensuring staff are recognized as a communication priority.

TOP TIP

Mapping the internal audiences can be done quickly if time has been invested in developing and testing the crisis communication plan. Identify which teams may have to work in difficult or challenging circumstances responding to the crisis and ensure that they are dealt with as a priority group. Then work through the employees to find the touchpoints such as staff officially using social media, frontline staff (e.g. those working in shops or meeting customers) and detail how, when and by whom they will be given information and be involved in the developing response.

Remember that staff will also be gathering information about the crisis through the external channels of communication, which may be both media and social media. Therefore, it is essential to ensure that the narrative is consistent across all communication activity, whether internal or external. Messages given to staff must be clearly aligned to the public statements that are made. If there is any discrepancy between them, it will be recognized and has the potential to impact negatively on trust and confidence in the business from the public and staff. Remember that staff will also be digesting the statements and interviews undertaken in the external communication after an incident. Ensure honesty and consistency are in place to maintain confidence. If you have developed a detailed crisis communication plan then you will potentially have identified ways in which the employees can review and support the communication activity, and they can provide a reality check for the messages that are going to be circulated both externally and internally. Employees can provide vital feedback on the communication, the response and the impact it is having at a time when opportunities for wider consultation are limited.

Messages: Getting the right words

Developing the narrative must take account of all the circumstances that are currently known and available to whoever is leading the communication. It will become the basis of all the communication activity and is one of the most important aspects of the work that is undertaken in response to a crisis. The messaging must provide enough detail so people can understand what is happening and know how they may need to respond or react. When dealing with the internal messaging the same principles of honesty, transparency and proactivity will apply.

Staff need to understand what situation the organization is facing and what it means for the business but more importantly for them as individual employees. They need to fully understand this so that they can work out the actions that need to be put in place within their area of the business. There are two elements that are in place as part of communication: operational and promotional. The operational element is the actions that are required to achieve a satisfactory conclusion to the crisis, and the actions that staff need to take. The promotional element is the messaging and narrative around the crisis that staff can help to share and explain to customers, stakeholders and others. Internal messages should be built on the narrative or core script with additional relevant staffing information provided. As stated, with all the messaging it is important to hit the right tone with what is said and how it is presented. At the heart should be an understanding of the impact of the issue or incident on the staff within the organization, and a recognition of the effort that will be required from employees to address the situation and move forward. Ensure the messaging is open and inclusive, talking with staff rather than talking at them. Imagine you are working in a small construction firm where a worker has been seriously injured. What is said to staff should take account of the upset there will be among colleagues and the potential for those who may have witnessed what happened to feel traumatized. It will be important to remember this and work with employees rather than to issue statements that appear insensitive.

There is often an expectation from management that employees will just continue to do their work without being affected by what has happened. But if the reputation of the business is going to be affected then it will have an impact on them and, as mentioned, potential future employees who will be assessing the way the organization responds. The incident will be talked about among employees' family and friends, which will reflect on them as members of the organization.

The success of the crisis response will be built upon the efforts of employees and this should continually be recognized within the communication messages. Being able to mention specific groups of employees or departments in statements and communication will also be beneficial to building confidence from workers that management fully understand what is taking place. If there are groups providing part of the early response or looking to get a grip of the issue that has occurred, then recognize their hard work. It will give them a boost but also demonstrate that management are supporting employees and are aware of the impact of the incident or issue. This recognition can be part of the internal statements. There is also an opportunity to highlight this by showing the work that staff are doing behind the scenes to manage the crisis. This can build confidence within people looking at the response and activity, and also highlight and recognize the work of employees involved.

Internal messaging must cover many areas, which can lead to lengthy statements being drafted. It is more beneficial to split the messaging so that it is in digestible chunks. If you have mapped your employees so that you can identify relevant areas of communication, then targeting messages to them will be easier. Dealing with the crisis is taking the staff on a journey, so help them to build understanding and momentum rather than throwing everything at them and expecting they will be able to make sense of it in one go.

Ensure the internal communication activity has covered:

- details of the issue or incident;
- the action that the organization is taking to deal with the situation and what the priority activities are;
- what is expected from staff at the current time and how they can support the work that is taking place;
- how staff can find support if they are struggling due to the nature of the issue or incident or because of the work they have been involved with in the response;
- details of how further information will be communicated to them, by what method and at what time.

The issue of the welfare and support that should be referenced and included in internal communication will be covered in more detail in Chapter 7.

All internal communication messaging should be personable and from a recognized and identified senior leader or the CEO. Remember the lead for employee engagement could be the HR manager, so ensure they are named on statements so they are seen to be leading. Statements that are issued without connection to a person become impersonal and distance the leadership from the frontline staff, which should be avoided when a crisis hits. Everyone needs to be working together to find a way forward. Remember to consider what staff will take from and feel about the communication that is provided. As the situation develops, having them involved or able to quality assure the messaging and activity will be beneficial to being effective. If you have the structure that has been outlined where managers and leaders across the organization have responsibility to be part of the communication network, then bring them in at an early stage to provide a briefing and discuss the messaging. Listen to them and encourage them to gather more views and provide feedback during the crisis and into the recovery phase. It is the data and analysis that can help ensure there is continued authenticity in the communication and that it is meeting not only the organization's needs but those of the employees.

Developing plans for the messaging in the future is vital and should happen in the early stages of the response once the initial pressure has subsided slightly. Always try to be looking ahead considering what may happen and how you can manage the communication around it. Use the data and information that you have about the employees' views and the issues they are facing, and any operational information will be crucial to this understanding, to develop long-term employee engagement plans. This will be vital as you move through the initial phase into recovery. For many crises that are encountered the impact can run for a long time, sometimes lasting for many years, with debriefs, reviews, inquiries, reports and analyses that all have the potential to negatively impact on the employees. This is covered in Chapter 8, looking at long-running crises and recovery. There needs to be a structure and approach that are agreed and ready to put in place when a trigger event happens, to ensure staff are remembered.

Evaluating the impact

The challenge to communication activity is being able to evaluate the impact that it has had, and this is still the case in a crisis. There is no simple method of undertaking evaluation and each business will have its own standard methods for evaluating how communication, both internal and external, is working. What matters is that you have outlined and put in place procedures to gather data and insight that will support the evaluation that needs to take place. In establishing the aims and objectives of the crisis communication plan you need to identify how you will analyse whether you have achieved what you set out to do. At this point it is important to remember to put SMART objectives in place. Identify a focus that is specific, measurable, achievable, relevant and time bound. Putting these in place at the planning stage will support the evaluation process. Also ensure you are clear when the evaluation will take place. For a long-running crisis that takes place over many months or years there will be key milestones and points along the way where evaluation is required to assess the impact and look at the change that may be required in the communication approach. In shorter crises it may be appropriate only to evaluate the impact once the situation is under control. The review of the impact should be kept at the forefront of considerations when managing crisis communication.

There are two types of data: qualitative and quantitative. In understanding how successful your internal communication activity is, you will need to have both. It may be that you have a strand of the work that is focused on employee wellbeing and making staff aware of what support is available to assist them. In this case the statistics on the number of staff taking up those opportunities will assist in the evaluation of the impact. But you also need to know what the level of understanding is about the incident and the response and what it means for the employees. Not all of that information will be forthcoming when just looking at the numbers reached. Instead, take the opportunity of organizing a focus group of staff or going out and talking to them. You can then dip sample the awareness of the messaging that was issued, assess what action it led the employees to take and gather views on the morale of the employees.

If you are not already aware of the Barcelona Principles developed by the International Association for the Measurement and Evaluation of Communication (AMEC)[1] then it is worth reviewing them and considering both your daily business and how they may assist evaluation during a crisis. This will require a focus on outputs, outtakes, outcomes and the organizational impact of the work that has been carried out (see below). A baseline is required, and this should utilize data and information that is in place before the crisis happens. Start by considering the inputs, activities and objectives that you had in place, before moving to the evaluation of the impact. Consider the four Os:

Outputs – these are the communication that you put out publicly or share with staff. Consider who received it and who was the intended audience. This can be measured through looking at the internal email, intranet, staff events.

Outtakes – what the staff did with the things that you shared and what they took from the communication. This could be measured by looking at dip sampling awareness and understanding of the messages.

Outcomes – this element considers the effects on the staff and whether there has been any change in attitudes or behaviour. This can be measured through reviewing trust and confidence in the organization's approach and activities.

Organizational impact – this is the ultimate benefit of the communication work that is undertaken, to the organization and its goals and objectives. This can be assessed through the data that is held within the business, including retention of staff and the tangible achievement of the goals that are outlined.

Organizations should have methods in place to track employee morale, sickness and advocacy rates that can be assessed and compared over time. This will be essential insight that will allow a detailed communication plan to be developed to support the recovery of the business. Track whether the crisis and any subsequent aftermath had an impact on the rates of support for the business. What does it mean for the senior managers and leaders of the business? What does it mean for the communication team and the activity they have underway? How can you take the insight and improve the ongoing employee engagement work? A crisis has the potential to have a long-term impact on all those associated with the business, but communicators must understand what that is and what it means, as this will then inform future activities, plans and developments.

The future for staff

Dealing with a crisis can take its toll on employees, specifically those managing the aftermath. Having effective communication in place focused on employee engagement, not just telling people information but listening, should be a priority for the communication teams and the leadership of the business. The communication staff have a balancing act to achieve as they must ensure enough time and resources are dedicated to the conversation with employees and not just the demands of media and social media. However, successful crisis communication can only be achieved with a holistic approach that brings all the activity together in one plan. This ensures consistency and clarity across all the communication activity and can define where resources are allocated.

Planning will ensure you are able to have the right systems and processes in place to achieve the integrated approach to communication from the moment a crisis emerges. The structures will support and assist this work. Leadership will recognize the responsibility to deliver effective employee communication that embodies the values of the organization and includes listening to staff, their views and issues.

Any crisis is likely to be a long-term issue for the business. It will appear, reappear and re-emerge at points in the future. Communication teams must attempt to identify the trigger points for it to reappear, and plan accordingly. It will ensure leaders are alerted and able to develop the appropriate response. Increasingly this will include the support for the wellbeing of staff. A crisis will test resilience at all levels and ensuring the wellbeing of the staff will support the future development of the business. Reputations are won or lost through effective actions and handling of a crisis. If staff are supported and cared for it will assist with the recruitment and retention of employees. Without it there is a possibility that staff will publicly voice their concerns about the internal handling of the crisis, which will intensify the pressure of the situation being managed.

Employees are fundamental to the effective response to a crisis and should be central to the crisis communication strategy and the associated plans. Get it right with employees and you are more likely to create an effective crisis communication strategy.

CASE STUDY
P&O industrial dispute

On 17 March 2022, P&O Ferries took the controversial step of sacking 800 employees with immediate effect. The move was criticized by the UK Government, which called for the CEO of P&O Ferries to appear before the Transport Select Committee a week later.[2] New crew members were brought in, and services were halted as they required training. New crews were made up of foreign workers being paid below the minimum wage.

Communication to staff affected consisted of a prepared video message, which was shown to staff who were then escorted off the ships. Later in the day the company released a statement, which said that in its current state the business was not viable. It added: 'Our survival is dependent on making swift and significant changes now. Without these changes there is no future for P&O Ferries. These circumstances have resulted in a very difficult but necessary decision, which was only taken after seriously considering all the available options. As part of the process, we are starting today, we are providing 800 seafarers with immediate severance notices and will be compensating them for this lack of advanced notice with enhanced compensation packages.'[3]

CEO Peter Hebblethwaite told the Committee that the company had acted outside of the UK law but stated that he would do it again.[4] He said the action was required to save the company but the comments at the Committee led to calls for his resignation.[5] Shortly after this happened one of the first ships with new crew was detained in Northern Ireland as the Maritime and Coastguard Agency said there were 'failures on crew familiarization, vessel documentation and crew training'.[6]

The job losses led to a number of reviews considering what could be done about the situation. One of these reported in the Summer 2022 update from the Insolvency Service concluded that there was 'no realistic prospect of a conviction' so they would not begin criminal proceedings.[7,8] Despite the situation P&O Ferries' parent company DP World posted record profits for the first half of 2022 at $721 million (£604 million). This was a 51 per cent increase, which the company said had come as they focused on shipping cargo with higher profit margins.[9]

Key learning points

- Ensure that being human is at the centre of your communication approach. The way you treat people affected by a crisis will be a significant factor in the way the response is judged. In this situation the video message may have been practical, but it demonstrated a lack of empathy with the employees. The situation is exacerbated when the business is the source of the change or issue.

- Plan and prepare for business changes and announcements. Difficult and challenging situations can be more effectively managed if they are subject to careful planning and consideration ahead of any implementation.

- No organization should appear arrogant in its response to an internal crisis as it can leave reputational damage. Taking an open and honest approach is an essential part of effective crisis communication. Losing a positive reputation can impact on recruitment, staff retention, customers and stakeholders. It also ensures the media spotlight will remain on the business for some time, putting all operations and decisions under intense scrutiny.

- In this situation, working carefully with stakeholders to alert them to the problems the company faced, then building to the potential for redundancies would have helped to manage the impact of the announcement.

- The crisis does not end when you say it ends. Many months after the situation the investigations and other announcements including those about company profits put the business back under pressure. In the case of P&O Ferries it led to further calls for the CEO to resign. Preparing ahead and considering the long-term impact of the crisis on people and the business is essential.

Conclusion

The human cost and impact of the crisis on people is the most important aspect of the situation to consider when developing the communication response. The way that people are dealt with, both the employees and those affected, will be fundamental to whether it is seen to be a positive response from the organization. Employee engagement is the foundation to any successful organization and valuing staff remains important throughout the incident and into the recovery phase.

It is more than just telling staff what is happening and providing instructions; to be truly effective you should involve employees in the crisis planning, approach, delivery and recovery. Part of this is to ensure that staff are educated in both the crisis response and the communication approach. They need to understand it and what their role is in relation to it. This includes how they may be discussing the situation, both with colleagues and publicly, including on social media. Employees must recognize that their actions both at work and at home can impact on the crisis response.

The internal communication activity requires a senior leader to be working with the communication team, providing leadership and ensuring it is driven at the top level, and seen to be as important as the external communication and work with the media. The right person taking this role will mean that swift actions and decisions can be taken, and resources can be provided to support those working in this area.

Understand the channels that you have access to, what works, who it reaches and whether it is trusted as a source of information. Use this to focus the internal activity on those who are the most appropriate for the circumstances of the crisis. But ensure that no matter what channel you are using, whether it is internal or external, the communication messages and narrative are consistent.

Finally, the employee communication must link to, and work closely with, the welfare response that is in place to support the affected employees. Staff that feel supported and cared for by the organization are more likely to be aligned to the business and will voluntarily give extra effort to the work that is required.

Notes

1   AMEC. Barcelona Principles 2.0, 2015. www.amecorg.com (archived at perma.cc/DU4U-6H4W)

2   M Weaver and P Walker. Downing Street urges P&O Ferries boss to resign after 800 sackings, *Guardian*, 25 March 2022. www.theguardian.com/business/2022/mar/25/po-ferries-boss-should-quit-after-brazen-mass-sackings-says-shapps (archived at perma.cc/UD8Q-KY2B)

3   ITV News Meridian. P&O Ferries sacks 800 staff as part of 'necessary' cuts and replaces them with agency workers, 17 March 2022. www.itv.com/news/meridian/2022-03-17/p-and-o-ferries-suspends-all-sailings-ahead-of-major-announcement (archived at perma.cc/9DDV-PX9G)

4   K Gilchrist. Britain's P&O Ferries broke the law in laying off 800 staff, boss admits, CNBC, 24 March 2022. www.cnbc.com/2022/03/24/britains-po-ferries-broke-the-law-in-laying-off-800-staff-boss-says.html (archived at perma.cc/9M98-ZATP)

5   J Meierhans. Calls for P&O Ferries boss Peter Hebblethwaite to resign grow. BBC News, 25 March 2022. www.bbc.co.uk/news/business-60872294 (archived at perma.cc/6594-QCG9)

6   M Badshah. P&O ferry detained over crew training concerns, says coast-guard agency, *Guardian*, 25 March 2022. www.theguardian.com/business/2022/mar/25/po-ferry-detained-over-crew-training-concerns-says-coastguard-agency (archived at perma.cc/V3K3-JN94)

7   BBC News. P&O Ferries won't face criminal action over mass sacking of staff, 20 August 2022. www.bbc.co.uk/news/uk-62613625 (archived at perma.cc/T4Y2-898H)

8   The Insolvency Service. P&O Ferries: update from the Insolvency Service, GOV.UK, 19 August 2022. www.gov.uk/government/news/po-ferries-update-from-the-insolvency-service-19-august-2022 (archived at https://perma.cc/UE3J-KJTL)

9   J Duggan. P&O Ferries: Grant Shapps calls for travel firm's boss to resign over mass sacking of 800 seafarers, *i News*, 19 August 2022. www.inews.co.uk/news/p-and-o-ferries-grant-shapps-travel-boss-mass-sacking-seafarers-1803851 (archived at https://perma.cc/7U4M-B8UC)

5

It's tough at the top: The role of leadership in a crisis

An essential ingredient for successful crisis management is the presence of strong and effective leadership. It isn't just the person at the top of the business who needs to demonstrate leadership skills; it must be shown at every level of the structure for the response to the crisis. We discussed the structure for dealing with a crisis in Chapter 1. Each person with responsibility for delivering an element of the response must espouse the qualities required to help the organization through the crisis, into recovery and on into a secured future.

In the previous chapter we discussed how confidence in management from the employees is an important factor in the crisis communication response. This confidence must be built with the leadership approach that is in place throughout the issue or incident. If employees have trust in the people managing them and feel they are being given the right information and know what to do, then it can start to build confidence. This must be information that is beneficial and relevant to them. Leadership is about more than purely having an effective system in place where plans are developed and disseminated. It is more than just managing the situation. There are qualities required in each leader to help steer the organization through the challenging circumstances.

Driving the crisis response

Responding to a crisis needs to be done swiftly and plans that have been developed to assist the organization to be in a state of readiness need to be implemented. The CEO of the organization, or the equivalent role such as managing director, must be made aware of the situation at the earliest opportunity. They must be among the first to be alerted to ensure they can mobilize the right people and ensure processes are put in place to develop the operational response. It is why the CEO must be involved in both the crisis planning and risk management work that is undertaken. This is good business housekeeping. The most senior person in the business should be driving the company to have a state of operational readiness to face any circumstances that may arise. It is also true that whatever the CEO of a business is interested in or concerned with will get the focus of the rest of the employees. This means that if they show an interest in the work to develop risk management and crisis planning, the rest of the business will prioritize it.

Given the crucial role that the CEO has working alongside the communication team during a crisis, they need to have been through exercises and tests of the plans that have been developed. They have very specific activities to undertake, as well as being in the spotlight with the public, employees, media, social media and others, who will all be looking in detail at what they do and how they do it as the crisis unfolds.

If they don't understand the requirements of the role of CEO in a crisis, if they lack the skills and qualities, or they lack accountability to step forward into the spotlight, then it will have a significant and detrimental impact on the response. For the communicator attempting to work with a CEO who is not engaged with this area of work during a crisis it will be a very challenging uphill struggle. The communication will be affected if there is not strong crisis leadership in place. But the communicator and communication team can help to bring this issue to the forefront when developing a crisis communication strategy and use it to review the leadership capabilities. Be clear about the communication requirements from the CEO and other senior leaders when developing the crisis communication plan. It may be that additional training or shadowing is required to build the skills and resilience within the managers across the business. All this work can be undertaken as part of the planning, reviewing and testing of crisis plans.

Crisis leadership qualities

There are 10 key leadership qualities that need to be evidenced to support effective crisis communication. A leader who can demonstrate them all will put the organization in a more advantageous position, and this should be something that all those leading organizations are seeking to achieve.

The 10 qualities are:

1 Motivating
2 Consistent
3 Decisive
4 Compassionate
5 Visible
6 Ethical
7 Resilient
8 Responsible
9 Effective at communicating
10 Skilful at managing expectations

Motivating

The world will be watching the leader of a business when it is affected by a crisis and everything they do and say will be analysed. Affected people, customers and those involved want to have the confidence that things are being effectively managed. Employees of the business want to feel they are being given support to do what is required to tackle the situation. All this requires the leader to be positive and to take people with them, creating an atmosphere where staff feel they will get through the challenging times. This can be achieved by the leader demonstrating that they are leading from the front, and they understand the impact of what staff are facing. A positive approach, where the leader also consistently appears to be unflustered by whatever twists and turns the crisis takes, will benefit everyone. It builds confidence and with that, employees will continue to do what is required, safe in the knowledge that it will move the organization and the situation forward.

Consistent

The importance of having a clear and consistent narrative about the crisis that is understood across the business has been outlined in previous chapters. Consistency is an important way to build confidence in the response. The leader can achieve this by embodying the brand values of the business. Organizations can move away from the principles the business operates under when an issue or situation develops. This is the easy option and will require fewer difficult decisions to be made. However, it is when the organization is under pressure that it needs to stick closely to the vision and ethos that it stands for. This will be understood by employees and customers alike and gives them some certainty during the moments of pressure. If the leader at the top of the business is seen to embody the brand values, then others will follow, which will build consistency across the organization and most importantly within the communication as part of the response.

Decisive

Responding to a crisis requires swift action, which means quick decisions need to be made. The leader needs to show they are in control and are comfortable to take those decisions that will put actions in place. This is not a time to waver and appear nervous about the task that is ahead. It is why the leader needs to have been involved in the crisis planning so they are able to move quickly into taking a decisive role directing the response because they know the plan in detail. The response must be swift but never appear hurried because haste brings a flustered appearance and lack of control, and that in turn impacts on confidence. A true leader will be able to listen to advice and guidance that may be given by experts within the business and will show how they are using that guidance to inform the actions that are being taken. There is a careful balance that must be struck between being directive and finding a way to be able to involve staff in the development of plans. It is particularly important for the leader to show they have listened to and heard the views of affected people, employees and members of the public. A failure to listen and ensure a course of action is in place will extend the lifetime of the crisis.

Compassionate

Historically, the public expectation of a CEO during a crisis was that they would show resilience, calm and that they were taking action. These elements are all still important but alongside this there is an expectation of some humanity coming through the communication and activity. We can see the authentic and compassionate voice come through from New Zealand Prime Minister Jacinda Ardern[1] in response to the terrorist attack in 2019, covered in the case study at the end of this chapter, or from the CEO of Alton Towers in 2015 when the focus of his response was on those injured in the roller-coaster incident. People want to see that the emotion of the issue or incident has been understood right to the top of the organization. We see this in further detail in some of the case studies throughout this book, particularly Alton Towers, discussed in Chapter 8. When public statements are being made it is vital that they reflect an understanding of the human cost of the issue or incident. Facts should not exist without emotion and emotion should not exist without facts when developing statements and messages about a crisis situation. It also means that the leader needs to be able to show empathy and humanity visibly in media interviews or any TV/video footage. Without some emotion being evident the response will appear cold and impersonal. However, they should not be viewed as hysterical in their approach, which means another careful balancing act must be in place. CEOs should allow their human response to the issue or incident to assist in shaping the response, and if they do it with authenticity it will appear as an acceptable form of emotion. The CEO must be approachable, recognize the importance of the public response and deal with things as a human being and not just the person in charge of the business.

Visible

A CEO who is not visible from the early stages of a crisis will be viewed as hiding from the problem, which will reflect on the organization's response. As we have seen, a swift recognition that there is a crisis emerging or underway is vital to show situational awareness and increase confidence that action is being taken. This visibility needs to be in place throughout the duration of the crisis with the key groups that have been outlined in plans, both public and staff. It does create additional pressure on the CEO who is already facing a huge burden of responsibilities, but there are other aspects of the response that can be delegated to prioritize communication and being visible. The CEO must utilize methods of communication to show they are involved in the response, are directing events, but are also listening to views and meeting with those affected. If another senior manager is being used for communication that is fine, but at some point the CEO must be seen to speak. Face-to-face communication with key staff who have been affected or are heavily involved in the response is a vital part of the employee engagement work. The same is true for key external groups and individuals, including any victims, victims' families, affected people, stakeholders and shareholders. It is an onerous task but one that is a key step towards effective crisis management and moving towards recovery. At the heart of the communication plan is that the CEO has a vital role as the face of the organization and must step up to do this at some point in the early stages of the crisis.

Ethical

The leader must be focused on doing the right thing in developing the response to the crisis and not on trying to protect the reputation of the company. In 2006, two young children died in a hotel in Corfu due to carbon monoxide poisoning. The tour operator, Thomas Cook, faced significant criticism for its treatment of the family and finally apologized after the inquest in 2015.[2] Some form of apology could have been given much earlier. A similar accusation could be levelled at the leaders running Oxfam at the time of the sexual exploitation allegations were made in 2018 (see the case study in Chapter 3). Demonstrating an ethical approach is closely aligned to the humanity that is an essential part of how the leader operates. The business must operate within any ethical or legal frameworks and ensure the decision making is undertaken in line with these. But it goes further than that – there is the court of public opinion to consider. Organizations and leaders who put protecting the reputation of the business as the top priority will make bad decisions based on flawed logic. They will act based on facts and figures but at the expense of the emotion of the situation. The approach should be based on doing what is required to get through the crisis effectively while ensuring that the people involved are supported. Again, in developing the action that is required, consider how it will be viewed by people outside the business. This is where the monitoring of media, social media and the views of the employees is vital in assisting the planning. It is a crucial service that the communication team can provide to the CEO and leadership team.

FIGURE 5.1   Example of a reputation tracker

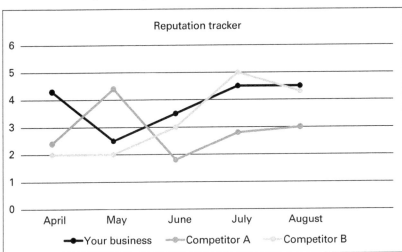

Resilient

Dealing with a crisis is exhausting and it will be the most pressured time in any leader's working life. The leader has an opportunity to deal effectively with the situation and build their credibility in the role. The same is true for the communication team who can build a positive reputation through their handling of the crisis. But it can also break them and the leader, damage their reputation and ultimately put them out of a job. Leaders need to work on their own development to ensure that they have the inner strength to face the challenges and work through them. They need to appear as the face of the organization as well as directing the activity and working out long-term plans for recovery. It is a time of immense pressure that they cannot show as they must maintain a level of composure throughout. This doesn't mean that they should neglect their own psychological wellbeing as they, like all affected by potentially traumatic circumstances, should ensure they seek appropriate help. This will be covered in Chapter 7 when we will look at resilience and wellbeing in more detail.

Responsible

A crisis, as we have seen, will put a huge pressure on the leader of the organization. They face operational demands, communication requests and stakeholders that require managing. Everyone will want to get a piece of them during the crisis response. There will be demands for the CEO to carry out media interviews, union leaders will want reassurances for the employees of the business and politicians, business leaders and banks will all need to be engaged with. This cannot be achieved by one person alone and the crisis response team or the network of strategic and tactical leads is essential to deliver the response. Effective crisis management is built on effective teamwork, but the leader must take responsibility. If there is a difficult decision to be made, then they need to be the one to make it. If there is an apology that needs to be made to affected people, then they need to do it. They are the person who is accountable for the issues or incident but more importantly for the organization's response to it. This means they need tactical advisers for areas of work, with communication as one area, and they need to prioritize their activities to ensure they are focusing on the most important tasks that need to be carried out. They must also manage their time effectively, which makes the role of their personal assistant in managing their diary a key part of the response framework.

Effective at communicating

All CEOs and senior leaders in organizations must understand the importance of effective communication to support the business. It means the communication team must demonstrate how they are effectively contributing to the business priorities daily. This work will assist when a crisis occurs, and the CEO or a senior manager must become the key spokesperson for the organization. A leader needs to not only understand the role of communication but they need to be an effective communicator. They need to be able to speak to people at all levels and across all sectors of society. They need to be able to undertake the most challenging of media interviews, and they need to know how to conduct themselves on social media. The latter element is important, as many CEOs and senior leaders are regularly using social media to engage with customers, service users and employees. How they behave on social media during the crisis, including whether they continue to post or not, will be subject to intense scrutiny.

Skilful at managing expectations

If the CEO has been able to share the narrative and engage with people throughout the early stages of a crisis then they will build trust and confidence in not just the business but in them as the leader of the business. This is built through an honest and open style that provides information based on evidence. They should manage the expectations not just of the public but also of employees. If the situation is going to take some time to bring under control, then they should say so with an explanation of why that is. If they require additional specialist skills to help to deal with the issue, then again explain this with the details of why. If the person at the top of the organization provides this level of information with an honest approach it will lead to trust and confidence in the response.

The right image

The 10 qualities show that the way the leader operates, the decisions that are made and the words that are used are vital to the success of the communication response. Remember we are in a visual world where the way someone presents themselves is still a key factor in how they are viewed by both the public and the media. Managing the image of the person in charge is not just important during the response to a crisis, it is part of the daily work of the communication team. It may seem that this should not be important to the crisis response but how the CEO appears is seen as a reflection of the health and wellbeing of the organization. They are viewed as the leader or representative of employees.

TOP TIP

Simple things can make a big difference. A carefully ironed shirt and appearing neat and tidy are ways to show visually that someone is in control. Attention should be given to the detail of the image that is presented. First impressions still count both when appearing before the media and in other interactions. If the leader is doing a TV interview, look at how the camera is framing them and ensure it presents the right picture. If they are talking to employees, ensure that they accurately reflect what is happening and explain the role staff need to play. Depending on the crisis that has emerged it may be more appropriate to choose a particular backdrop for such messages. These backgrounds may be at certain venues, be with specific people or provide confidence through being alongside other agencies.

The image does not always have to be 100 per cent strong and in control as mentioned when discussing the qualities; there can be some humanity, empathy and vulnerability presented by the leader. In considering this, the discussion must take account of the circumstances of the crisis, the role of the business in creating and managing the crisis, and the external tone and mood towards the crisis. Use all this information to consider what the best approach would be regarding strength and vulnerability. For example, if the organization is partly responsible for the problem and is going to make an apology, then ensuring that the understanding of the human impact comes through is critical. However, if the organization is not going to accept responsibility, then appearing to be emotional will lack authenticity and be seen as a cynical ploy to gather support. Therefore, the ethical strand of the qualities of leadership and communication must always be in place.

Image is also important, as are the words that are used and the personal delivery of the communication. Above all, authenticity must be in place with a personal twist. Communicators can draft statements, answers and narratives but if something is going to be attributed to the leader then that person must be comfortable that it reflects how they would speak. They need to develop a personal connection to the wording and presentation so a constructive dialogue about it can exist. The communicator and the leader of the business should have developed a working relationship before the crisis that will allow this discussion to take place in an open and frank way. The communicator must have the freedom and support to be able to provide advice and guidance, and the leader needs to be comfortable with the nature of the conversation. Ultimately, a leader who has considered the clothes to wear and the way to look, along with developing a personal connection to what they are going to say, is likely to demonstrate authenticity and increase confidence in the response.

Training leaders in communication

The look of the company spokesperson is important, but it is also essential for them to have been effectively trained to deal with media interviews, community meetings, stakeholder and shareholder meetings and employee engagement. This training is vital to develop the business as the head or executive team are running the organization and will be put under the spotlight during a crisis. It is often a neglected area of work for many reasons, including budgetary or time pressures or an unwillingness from those at the top to undertake media and communication training. Being able to sensitively sell senior managers the proposition of training is something that the lead communicator in the organization will need to do. It is why skills such as influencing and negotiation must be key parts of the abilities of the modern communicator. Consider such skills in any training plan or professional development work. When a crisis hits, the pressure quickly mounts on the person at the head of the business and they must be able to respond swiftly, which means having all the necessary skills in place. Take time now to be ready to respond in the future. The leadership team must be involved in the development of the crisis communication plans and the testing of them, as outlined in Chapter 1. This will help to increase their readiness to deal with a crisis. But the training must go further than just an awareness of the crisis communication plan.

There is an element of performance that is required to manage the communication around a crisis, but this should not be a negative thing. With any performance there are rehearsals, people learn their lines, they look the part and then they are confident to face the audience. In the same way the crisis spokesperson must have exercised and reviewed the crisis communication plan and the organizational crisis management strategy, they should know the communication approach and the wording that may be used, they should know how they want to look in the event of interviews at a time of crisis, and should be trained so they feel able to face the communication challenges. Time spent in preparing, developing and training is time well spent. It will mean the CEO, senior managers and spokesperson are prepared and ready no matter what the crisis.

Who is the spokesperson?

In developing the spokesperson, we have focused primarily on the role being carried out by the head of the organization, but although this is what is usual it isn't always possible or appropriate. In some cases, the person at the top of the organization is so heavily involved in the crisis that they may be unable to act impartially, or they may not be seen as able to act honestly. In this situation you must ensure you have the right person with the right qualities, as outlined earlier in the chapter. Training the whole of the executive team to be able to undertake the role of spokesperson in a crisis is advisable. When considering the crisis media and communication training develop something that can be rolled out to all the top team. Bringing in specialist crisis communication advisers and trainers will allow this to be undertaken in a confidential and independent way. Many senior leaders will find it difficult to learn from a more junior member of staff. The communicator can act as a specialist intermediary working with both the communication and leadership teams.

The spokesperson must be able to commit a significant amount of time to undertake the required media and communication activities linked to the crisis. This includes undertaking media interviews, developing digital packages, going to see key employees and speaking to stakeholders. These responsibilities can be shared if the structure is put in place to support this, focusing on consistency of messages and a narrative that is clearly understood by all involved in communicating. If you are the CEO or managing director of a small company, you need to be able to call upon support to manage the response and the communication responsibilities. Think this through as part of the planning.

All those involved in being spokespeople will also have to make themselves readily available to the communication team. They should be able to be called upon at a moment's notice as the crisis develops or may erupt. Every organization needs to have a duty rota for incidents that happen out of office hours. This includes dealing with an emerging media issue so that the communication team can contact a senior person at a moment's notice during the day or night. This process should be written into the crisis communication plan as part of the structure to deal with the time a crisis happens and becomes known. But that level of access to senior leaders is essential throughout the crisis so that issues can be challenged, responses provided and the spokesperson can maintain the visibility that is required at all levels.

Understandably if a crisis runs for an extended period of time, as was seen with the Covid-19 pandemic, the spokesperson is unlikely to be the same person, as they will face burnout. Even if the crisis lasts for just 48 hours, as it will have a continuous requirement for communication it needs a spokesperson and a deputy to be established. The priority will be to keep the same face and use the same spokesperson wherever possible but if essential the deputy can be used. Both should have had the required media and communication training to deal with a crisis and should understand the detail of the crisis communication plan. A key to the effective working of this relationship is for them to have a detailed understanding of the plans and approaches, to have a confidence in their ability to communicate and to keep consistency and continuity with the organization's narrative in relation to the crisis.

The spokesperson is a key role and should be supported with advice and guidance throughout the duration of the crisis. This includes providing opportunities to undertake proactive communication through available channels including media interviews and livestreaming, recognizing rumours or inaccuracies that need to be challenged and guiding the development of the narrative as the crisis runs and changes. The communication team should be able to wrap this support around the spokesperson(s) quickly and continuously.

Supporting the spokesperson

The development of the crisis strategy for any organization should have a big focus on the structures that are in place to support effective decision making during the response. This is covered in detail in Chapter 3 where we considered the role of command and control and the approaches that can be taken to manage the operational response.

Having the right people in place to provide tactical advice is essential for leaders dealing with all elements of the crisis. The strategy, as has been said, should already have been outlined and be ready to put in place for any crisis no matter what the circumstances are. So, these tactical advisers will be the bridge between the strategy and the tactical activity that is required specific to the incident or issue being faced. One of these advisers will be the communication and PR lead for the business. Others will represent specific parts of the business and its operational activity, and possibly someone to lead on shareholder issues. Plans and procedures must recognize the role of tactical adviser and put them in place at the start of the crisis to help those making decisions. One of the most challenging issues is balancing the advice from the legal adviser against that of the communication and PR adviser. The first is focused on the best legal outcome for the business, which will be based on not accepting liability unnecessarily and on protecting the operation. However, the PR lead will be looking at the moral approach and ensuring the future reputation of the business remains positive. The potential battle between these two often conflicting positions makes it essential for the communicator to have a good working relationship with the legal team, and influencing skills to be able to effectively argue the position to make an apology or accept some form of responsibility. At the end of the day, it will be the leader at the top of the organization who will be faced with listening to the advice and deciding.

TOP TIP

Before going into a discussion with leaders about different approaches to a crisis, ensure you have evidence to support the course of action you are going to advocate. Legal representatives will bring case law to support them in their advice to those leading the crisis response. To be able to challenge the legal recommendations ensure you have case studies of previous crisis situations and communication responses, can evidence the appropriate action and manage any concerns about perceived risks in your approach.

Being a leader dealing with a crisis can be a very lonely place as you take control and aim to ensure you are making the right decisions. You do this all while under the media and social media spotlight. The person at the top of the business must have enough resilience to be able to absorb the pressure, keep a clear head for decision making and be able to demonstrate a personal understanding about the issue and its impact. It is the toughest test for any head of an organization and their future will depend upon the successful management of the incident. They need to remain positive to bring the team and the organization with them in working through the crisis and building a successful recovery. It is why they need to surround themselves with tactical advisers who can provide information to ensure they are fully briefed to make any required decisions. These individuals, as we have said, will hold expert knowledge, and can advise on options and possible outcomes within their area of expertise.

Negative communication and the use of terminology that will damage the business need to be banned from discussions and from any communication that is shared both internally and externally. There is an inevitability that if the leader talks about failing to manage the crisis it will transmit to the rest of the operational response and the organization, who will then be building towards failure. Throughout a crisis, only positive terminology should be used and accepted. If we remember the BP Deepwater Horizon crisis, the language used by the CEO complaining about the personal impact of dealing with the disaster caused significant problems for the response and recovery. On 20 April 2010 an explosion occurred at the oil rig offshore south east of Houston. It caused the death of 11 crewmen. Two days later on 22 April the rig sank, causing the largest oil spill in US waters. BP CEO at the time Tony Hayward made a number of statements during the crisis that were criticized, including downplaying the impact in the early stages. On 30 May he told a reporter, 'We're sorry for the massive disruption it's caused to their lives. There's no one who wants this thing over more than I do, I'd like my life back.' It was the comments about his own position that were viewed as selfish by all those affected and their families.[3]

The same occurred in 2022 with the comments from a police chief in the aftermath of the Uvalde school shooting. His comments to a journalist when he talked about the families who had been bereaved, about waiting for them to 'quit grieving' sparked anger.[4] Details are outlined in the case study at the end of this chapter.

Ensuring staff wellbeing

When a crisis happens, it will put huge pressure on those involved in the initial response who will feel the weight of acting quickly and decisively. There will also be people deployed to support victims and victims' families or who may be involved in other sensitive areas of work. There will be people keeping the business running despite the crisis and there will be employees who may be going through difficult times. All of these will need extra support and care to ensure they are protected throughout the crisis. Wellbeing is an essential part of the internal communication response when a crisis happens. It means having the right services available to provide support to employees who may be feeling the pressure. There are lots of services that can be accessed so understanding what is available is an important part of the preparations. Support could mean the need for an employee to see a psychologist, to undertake some form of talking therapy or just to have a chance to share views as part of a debrief.

The leader's role must be to ensure this support is available but above all to demonstrate empathy with any employees who feel they need to access this support either during the crisis, at the conclusion of the crisis or even in the months and years to come. It must not be seen as a sign of weakness for an employee to ask for help or support to manage the psychological impact of dealing with a crisis. The person at the top of the business has the responsibility of creating a culture where it is acceptable to ask for assistance and to access support services. The enlightened leader will make it known that they have received support or are going to access support services, so it is seen as normal and not unusual. This will be covered in more detail in Chapter 7.

Leaders must decide to stay and see things through or leave the business. This may seem stark but it is the reality of any significant crisis situation. There are lots of factors that will need to be considered before making the decision. Sometimes the situation is so devastating, and the business is seen to be responsible, it will only be a matter of time before there are calls for the person at the top to go. An effective leader will recognize when this is going to happen and where it may lead to long-term damage to the reputation of the business and will make the decision to leave. However, in most cases what is important is the person at the top taking responsibility and showing that they will be in charge to see things through to their conclusion. This will inspire confidence from the workforce as well as customers, shareholders, stakeholders and the wider public. Visible leadership ensures the crisis is managed and that building for the future is guaranteed. Leadership is when you continue to run the business through the crisis and into recovery even if you make the personal decision to leave once you have moved past the recovery phase.

Leader's checklists

There are two checklists outlined below. The first is to assist the leader facing the initial stages of a crisis, providing a simple list of points to consider and elements to have put in place. The second checklist is for long-term essentials of the response that should be in place. These elements affect the ability to deliver effective crisis communication.

FIRST HOURS CHECKLIST

- Ensure you have been fully briefed and understand the issue and its possible future development.
- Head to the 'war room' or operational hub from where the incident is being managed.
- Make direct contact with key stakeholders or shareholders to provide an early alert that the crisis has occurred.
- Ensure you have the right clothes to undertake any media interviews or attend any key meetings.
- Gather key tactical advisers together.
- Appoint a member of staff to provide support by monitoring required actions and ensuring they are communicated to the right person.

- Identify the affected groups and individuals so they can be referenced within the communication and be part of the future communication activity undertaken.

- Meet with the communication lead to agree the initial narrative and key messages.

- Walk through the operational areas of the business, if possible, to be visible and offer support to those on the frontline of tackling the issue or incident. If this cannot be done physically then ensure there are online opportunities to connect such as virtual drop-in sessions. These areas will be defined by the nature of the crisis. If this is a reputational issue, then being visible within the communication and PR office will be welcomed.

- Establish a meeting structure and timetable for regular updates to be provided to the leader.

FUTURE ACTIVITIES CHECKLIST

- Have a programme of visits in place, either in person or virtually, to speak to the most affected employees face to face and ensure all key departments are visited. Even if the visit has not happened, knowing that it is going to take place will benefit staff.

- Welfare services should be in place and details of how to access them communicated, as well as managers being encouraged to refer people for help if they have any concerns.

- Ensure a consequence management unit is in place and that stakeholder and shareholder briefings have been mapped.

- Instigate the programme to debrief the response and review the activity that was undertaken.

- Receive a review of the impact of the crisis on the reputation of the business.

- Evaluate the communication plan and ensure there is continued proactivity built into the ongoing communication approach.

- Establish a group of staff to take forward any recommendations from reviews and debriefs that will embed any changes that are required and track developments.

- Review the structure of the response and identify any areas for development, including recommendations on training and exercising of the plans that are required in the future.

- Ensure a continued open, transparent and positive approach to communication.

CASE STUDIES

New Zealand terror attack and Uvalde school shooting: What do they reveal about leadership in a crisis?

New Zealand attack

On 15 March 2019 there was a terror attack in New Zealand targeting mosques where worshippers were praying. Fifty Muslim worshippers were murdered in the attack, which was partly livestreamed on Facebook. The leadership of the country's Prime Minister Jacinda Ardern received widespread praise from across the world.

She very quickly appeared on television and made a strong statement on what had happened, which demonstrated strength as well as compassion. It was an attempt to be a unifying voice at a time when there would be concern and distrust between communities.

Her initial statement included these lines:

Our thoughts and our prayers are with those who have been impacted today. Christchurch was the home of these victims. For many, this may not have been the place they were born. In fact, for many, New Zealand was their choice.

The place they actively came to and committed themselves to. The place they were raising their families, where they were part of communities who they loved and who loved them. It was a place that many came to for its safety. A place where they were free to practice their culture and their religion.[5]

The words were very powerful and created a direct connection between the victims and their families, New Zealand and herself. Ardern consoled the victims and their families in person and in giving statements showed humanity when she appeared upset. She appeared at events to mourn those who died and respectfully wore a hijab. Ardern also offered to cover the funeral costs for the victims.

In a widely publicized move, she refused to speak the name of the man responsible for the attack so that he did not receive the notoriety that he craved. It was a position she continued to hold throughout the crisis. In addition to the initial response, she moved quickly to talk of reform to the New Zealand gun laws, which showed decisive action to make a difference and learn from the crisis.

Key learning points

- Remember the small things that demonstrate caring and compassion, such as Ardern wearing the hijab.
- As well as a positive response to the events the leader needs to be finding ways to learn from events and make changes.
- Keep those affected at the centre of your response and your communication about the incident.
- Leaders can show humanity and vulnerability and still be seen as strong and decisive.

Uvalde school shooting

Nineteen children and two teachers were murdered in a shooting at Robb Elementary School in Uvalde, Texas, USA on 24 May 2022. The situation emerged at 11.30am when a teacher called 911 to report a car crash and a man with a gun, who minutes later started shooting through classroom windows. Five minutes later three officers from Uvalde Police Department entered the school and a further four followed but found the door locked.[6]

At 11.41am a police sergeant and US border agents arrived, and the rest of the school was evacuated. Parents had to be held back by police as they tried to gain entry to the school. Moments later parents pleaded with police for officers to enter the building. By 12.03pm there was a 911 call from a child in the classroom, who called a further three times in the following 10 minutes. The child said people had died but some were still alive. It was 12.38pm when an ambulance arrived at the school and at 12.47pm a second child called 911 saying 'please send the police now'.

A Border Patrol Tactical unit officer used janitor's keys to unlock the door and after further shots were fired the gunman was killed. Police announced at 1.06pm the shooter had been stopped. The police released inaccurate information and faced significant criticism that they had been slow to respond and to tackle the gunman. Governor Greg Abbott said he had been 'misled' about the police response when he spoke at a press conference shortly after the shooting happened.[7] In the weeks that followed the police continued to defend their response and claimed officers risked their own lives without hesitation. Parents criticized the response as being chaotic and slow.[8]

The problems were compounded when the Uvalde Police Department chief Pedro Arredondo was challenged about not working with an investigation into the shooting by the Texas Department of Public Safety. He said more information would not be released and then said to the CNN reporter 'We're going to be respectful to the family,' he said. 'We're going to do that eventually. Whenever this is done and the families quit grieving, then we'll do that obviously.' This again led to outrage at the phrase 'quit grieving', which demonstrated a lack of humanity, empathy and compassion.[9]

In July a report by the committee of state legislators found 'systemic failures and egregiously poor decision-making'. It highlighted a lack of leadership and urgency and a 'lackadaisical approach' by authorities.[10] In August the police officer in charge of the law enforcement response, Pete Arredondo, had his contract terminated with immediate effect at a meeting of the Uvalde Consolidated Independent School District's board.[11]

Key learning points

- Information should be accurate and provided as swiftly as possible, particularly to those who are affected by events. With this situation there were complaints of inaccuracies, delays in information and mixed messages.

- People must be at the heart of the response, and with so many people affected the communication should have centred around an apology, reparation and support to the families and children.

- Language really does matter and the poor choice of words by the police chief will impact on those caught up in the emergency. All communicators or those delivering messages during a crisis should take care with the words they use and consider how they will be received by those affected by the situation.

- Those at the top of the business should be trained to effectively deliver crisis communication. They should have a strong background in crisis leadership and training to balance the demands that they will face. This includes managing uncertainty, dealing with inconsistencies and taking decisive action.

- Apologies are important and should be considered within all crisis communication plans. There are times when it is not relevant but where there has been a significant failure by the organization it is important to proactively say sorry. Where corrective action can be taken it should be done quickly and the error minimized. However, any apology should be genuine and be about more than just words; the actions taken are critical to demonstrate the sentiments in the statement.

- In planning for a crisis response, identify agencies that will also be involved and discuss approaches to communication. This will assist when a situation emerges and will help to coordinate the response. Organizations should help people make sense of what has happened and working together can assist this.

Conclusion

Every crisis requires strong leadership to be in place. But this is not just from the CEO or the person in charge of the organization; it is important for everyone managing staff at all levels across the business. Obviously the CEO has a critical role, even if they are not the spokesperson at the start of the crisis. Remember the CEO will have many responsibilities and may be unable to devote the required amount of time to the communication demands. They must speak about the crisis before the incident has progressed too far, otherwise they will face criticism for appearing to hide from the events. Involve the CEO in the crisis communication planning so that the role and actions can be discussed before any situation emerges.

There are 10 leadership qualities that are essential for the crisis communication response. Among them are the importance of consistency and that is grounded in a rational approach to the events. Emotion is acceptable because authenticity is essential to the response from the CEO or person at the top. Leaders need to understand and recognize the importance of communication in a crisis but also in ensuring that the response is ethical and not rooted solely in protecting the reputation of the business or them as a leader.

CEOs need to be trained and accept feedback on how to present themselves. They have one chance to make the right impression so preparation is key. Formal training is important alongside identifying strong and successful leaders who they can study who have communicated effectively.

Train a number of people to undertake the spokesperson role. The right person will be required and with the pressure on that activity there needs to be a group of people who are ready to undertake the role. Ensuring resilience of the people involved in the response and of the organization's approach is essential. The more people who are able to do the role, the easier it will be to find someone to act as spokesperson in the critical initial stage.

If you are a leader, be prepared to listen to advice and recognize the knowledge of those around you who can be trusted advisers. Use their experience and the elements of the crisis communication plan, such as checklists, to support and guide you. If you are a communicator, ensure that the crisis communication plan includes checklists, guidance and support for leaders at all levels and critically for the CEO.

Notes

1   B Britton. New Zealand PM full speech: 'This can only be described as a terrorist attack', CNN, 15 March 2019. www.edition.cnn.com/2019/03/15/asia/ new-zealand-jacinda-ardern-full-statement-intl/index.html (archived at perma.cc/ZPL6-L2BD)

2   J Bourke. Thomas Cook: From a tragedy to corporate disaster, *Independent*, 19 May 2015. www.independent.co.uk/news/business/analysis-and-features/ carbon-monoxide-deaths-from-a-tragedy-to-a-corporate-disaster-for-thomas-cook-10259735.html (archived at perma.cc/C2NY-6LM7)

3   T Jaques. Lessons from an oil spill: how BP gained – then lost – our trust, *The Conversation*, 22 April 2015. www.theconversation.com/lessons-from-an-oil-spill-how-bp-gained-then-lost-our-trust-40307 (archived at perma.cc/ JTB9-HCZP)

4   A Cooper, S Prokupecz and E Levenson. Uvalde school district police chief declines to answer CNN questions in first public comments in a week, CNN, 1 June 2022. www.edition.cnn.com/2022/06/01/us/uvalde-shooting-police-chief-pete-arredondo/index.html (archived at perma.cc/J4XN-WZ6X)

5   B Britton. New Zealand PM full speech: 'This can only be described as a terrorist attack', CNN, 15 March 2019. www.edition.cnn.com/2019/03/15/asia/ new-zealand-jacinda-ardern-full-statement-intl/index.html (archived at perma.cc/ZPL6-L2BD)

6   L Keay. Texas school shooting: The full timeline of police's response to massacre, Sky News, 28 May 2022. https://news.sky.com/story/texas-school-shooting-the-full-timeline-of-polices-response-to-massacre-12622366 (archived at perma.cc/7YHM-ESQV)

7 J Fechter and R Oxner. 'The wrong decision': Texas DPS says local police made crucial error as school shooting continued, *Texas Tribune*, 27 May 2022. www.texastribune.org/2022/05/27/uvalde-school-shooting-police-errors/ (archived at perma.cc/R7W9-MB4R)

8 BBC News US and Canada. Texas school shooting: Uvalde school police chief defends mass shooting response, 10 June 2022. www.bbc.co.uk/news/world-us-canada-61685119 (archived at perma.cc/SX97-GQ87)

9 A Cooper, S Prokupecz and E Levenson. Uvalde school district police chief declines to answer CNN questions in first public comments in a week, CNN, 1 June 2022. www.edition.cnn.com/2022/06/01/us/uvalde-shooting-police-chief-pete-arredondo/index.html (archived at perma.cc/J4XN-WZ6X)

10 BBC News US and Canada. Texas shooting: Uvalde report finds 'systemic failures' by authorities, 18 July 2022. www.bbc.co.uk/news/world-us-canada-62200507 (archived at perma.cc/GZD2-QQJS)

11 C Phillips and D Katz. Uvalde school police chief fired 3 months after botched response to school shooting, NPR, 24 August 2022. www.npr.org/2022/08/24/1119340765/uvalde-pete-arredondo-fired-school-police-chief-robb-elementary (archived at perma.cc/DQ3W-ZGXN)

6

The impact on the community: Managing the consequences

People judge the way organizations and businesses deal with a crisis and are heavily influenced by the way that affected people are treated. If you treat the people who have suffered because of the crisis well, whether it was as a result of something the business has done or not, then you will receive recognition for it. Society is about people and regardless of how efficiently you deal with the issue, if you have not taken into account the people involved and the ways in which they are affected it will not be effective crisis communication. It is vital to have understood who the affected people are within the incident or issue you face. Earlier in this book we looked at the crisis and its impact, likening it to a pebble being thrown into a still pond. The pebble hits and then leaves ripples that are strong close to the pebble but are weaker further away. This is the same for the impact of a crisis. There are those who will be directly affected by the issue or incident and are at the centre, but you cannot forget the impact on others around or on the fringes of the crisis. Organizations must ensure they are able to work with and support people while ensuring that the communication is respectful and sensitive to the situation.

Communication plans must be focused on the human aspects of the issue or situation that the business is dealing with. Failing to include this will impact on the effectiveness of both the response to the crisis and the move to recovery. In Chapters 1 and 3 we discussed the importance of looking at the community who will be affected by the crisis and its aftermath. This is where consequence management has a key part to play. In preparing for a crisis, the way consequence management will work and the support that will be available for those affected including victims and victims' families must be detailed. It is vital to have a clear understanding of what, or who, your organization's community or communities may be.

Who are the community?

Defining the community for your business and set of circumstances can be quite problematic. It requires work to have been carried out to map stakeholders, understand customers and identify scenarios before any crisis happens. Having an existing stakeholder map is an important part of everyday communication. When a crisis occurs it is a resource that can help you to progress quickly to identify those key individuals or groups that you need to engage with. Each of these must consider both the internal and external audiences and be regularly reviewed and updated to take account of changes. Changes can be to the product or services, in personnel or the environment the business is working within. The affected people can be defined in many ways, from being from a geographic location, already an existing community in some form, service users or those caught up in the incident or issue. There will also be the internal community to consider, which we outlined in Chapter 4, looking at the impact on the workforce. Identify those who may be adversely impacted by the crisis and others who may be key stakeholders to the response so that you can use the data and information to develop the most efficient plan.

All this information needs to be readily available and understood by those leading the communication response to the crisis. It is not something that can, or should, be done on the spur of the moment when the crisis has emerged and is developing. Preparation is key and gives the ability to move quickly, put structures in place and to start managing the impact of what has happened. The three key aspects of managing the consequences are: stakeholder mapping, customer definition and impact analysis. They are defined as follows.

Stakeholder mapping

This is the process of outlining who the key stakeholders are for the business. Stakeholders are simply those people or organizations who have an interest and influence within the business. In most cases they will be employees, investors, customers, suppliers, regulators or other interested groups. The situation can change depending on the sector that the business operates in, for example whether a private company or a public or governmental body. A stakeholder map is a visual representation of these groups, which makes it easy to group them under certain characteristics; again this will be of vital importance to developing the communication plan. They are usually characterized according to the level of interest they have in the business and the amount of power or influence they may have that could impact on the business. There are a range of processes that can be undertaken to carry out stakeholder mapping and you can involve specialist companies to do the work for you.

However, there are four key steps:

1 Identify the stakeholders
2 Analyse the stakeholders
3 Prioritize the stakeholders
4 Develop engagement with the stakeholders

In each of the maps (Figures 6.1 and 6.2) you can see four boxes. The top right is for those with influence and with a high level of interest. This group needs regular updates and engagement rather than broadcast communication. The bottom right is for those with influence but little interest and these require promotion-style communication. The top left is for those with interest but little influence, requiring regular communication, and the bottom left is for those with little interest or influence and you may provide minimal updates to these groups.

Customer definition

An analysis of the people who use the service or buy the product created by the business will inform the customer profile. This could

FIGURE 6.1   Example stakeholder map for public organizations

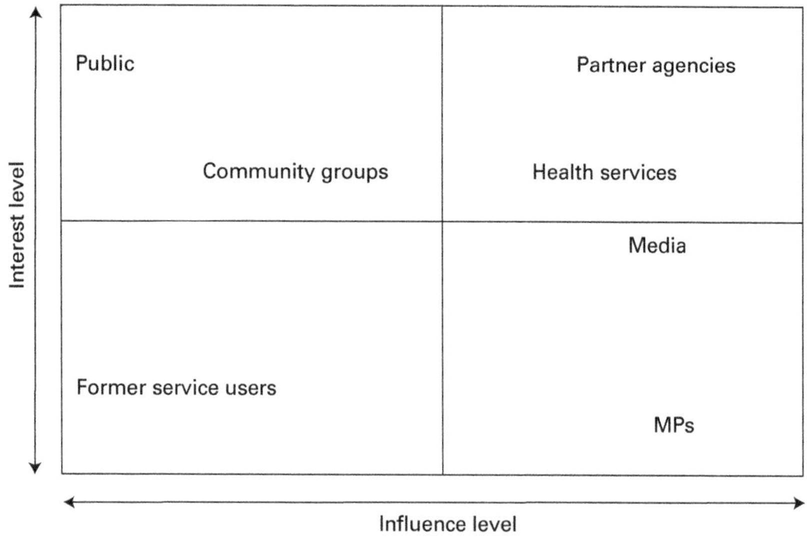

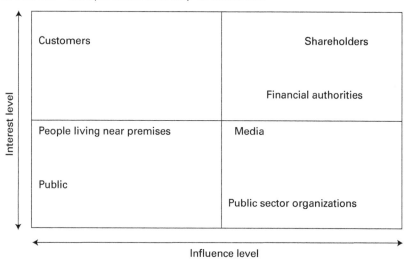

FIGURE 6.2   Example stakeholder map for businesses

involve the use of tools such as MOSAIC, which is a business model that uses extensive data sets to categorize people to increase the possibility of successful cross-channel communication. It was developed by Experian Limited and is used by many marketing departments. If this model or others are being used by the marketing department then discuss with them access to use it to benefit communication activity.

Systems can access significant amounts of data and then analyse them to provide a picture of the groups that can be classified as customers. Data and information that is available from customer services teams will also assist in developing this picture. The customer definition will always assist in targeting goods and services and is valuable not only at the point of a crisis emerging. The key is to understand who the customers and service users are and their likely characteristics, which allows improved targeting of communication. For example, if you are a small retailer operating in an specific location then you can understand how people access information to use this to target communication more effectively.

Impact analysis

This can, and should, be part of the risk management process that is in place for the business. It will look at the issues that may affect the organization and then consider how they could impact on the business at all levels. There will be statistical information and data to assist in the process but alongside this it requires qualitative data that will consider the customer experience and review similar issues that may have affected rival or competitor organizations. For each scenario that will have been considered and outlined as part of the planning and testing process there should be some form of impact analysis available.

The risk impact information is essential insight to support the development of a bespoke crisis communication approach for the problem at hand. When the situation emerges, refer to the work you have done and look at how it can assist in identifying who has been impacted by events, what you need to say to them and how to start saying it. Understanding the potential impact of scenarios is a vital part of the crisis preparedness work. For example, if you have considered the impact that a data loss or breach may have for the business, you will already understand the key connections to other organizations, who is affected and what it means to them. Considering this ahead of time helps in making swift progress.

Reputational issues have to be played into this process. If it is left to the accountants and lawyers then it will focus on financial and legal aspects but fail to take account of the impact that an issue may have on the reputation of the business. As we have discussed in Chapter 2, the impact of a reputational issue can be serious enough to lead to the end of the business or significant financial losses. Communicators have an important role to play in reviewing and updating the impact analysis to ensure it captures these factors.

Think bespoke

Once an issue or incident has occurred and a crisis is on the horizon the three elements must be reviewed and updated considering the specific circumstances that are being faced. This will help to define the community, and individuals, that are affected by the situation. In preparing communication, the narrative and any materials must take account of the groups that have been identified. A 'one size fits all' approach will only be acceptable in the very short-term initial stages of the crisis being declared. Very quickly after that, as we have already outlined, the organization should have a plan in place to deal with the situation at hand. Within this the communication can start to be targeted to reach the audiences that have been outlined.

It is important to remember to consider all aspects of the diverse communities and individuals that will be involved in the communication plan. With the speed of communication in the initial stages of a crisis it is easy to forget to consider diversity, so ensure that you have reviewed it in the planning and preparation for a crisis.

Ensure inclusivity

Crises intensify situations. If there is a challenge in connecting with audiences ahead of a crisis then it will only become more problematic when you are dealing with events. The crisis puts a spotlight on the effectiveness of communication. When crises emerge they have the ability to exacerbate inequalities that may exist within communities or society. This has been discussed in academic studies of the Covid-19 pandemic and the impact it had on increasing inequalities. One study featured in the Proceedings of the National Academy of Sciences of the United States of America, identified that: 'Crises lay bare the social fault lines of society. In the United States, race, gender, age and education have affected vulnerability to Covid-19 infection' and concluded with the point that 'Strategically deployed relief efforts and longer-term policy reforms are needed to challenge the perennial and unequal impact of disasters.'[1] So, our communication needs to consider diversity, equality and inclusivity from the moment we have to acknowledge the crisis has happened.

Start by understanding exactly who is affected by what has happened. Which communities may be at the heart of the crisis? Communities do not have to be about just geographic locations but can be around a theme, issue or interest. Who are these communities? Where are they based and how do they receive information? Even more importantly what sources of information do they trust? These questions will help you to ensure that you gather the required detail to move on to considering the communication that may be required. Remember that you will be considering the situation from your own perspective and viewpoint. This means you will assess what has happened from the point of view of your own knowledge and experience, and this may also be influenced by the organization you are working for. Gathering alternative perspectives and listening to different voices about the crisis, the impact of it and what it means for different communities is essential insight to gather as soon as practicable.

When you have identified who is affected consider what data and insight there is about them. How have they reacted to previous crises? Are they already connected to the communication from the business? Do they care about the issue that has emerged? If there is no relevant research and data that can assist, consider undertaking some insight gathering of your own. Look at what quick consultation could be done, or how a third party may be able to develop the necessary insight.

Once the information is available you can review and consider how this refocuses your communication. Are there communities that need to be a priority for you? What groups don't connect with the business but are affected by what has happened? This should then shape your communication towards becoming more inclusive in its approach. During the Covid-19 pandemic the UK Government needed to refresh and refocus its communication, which was attempting to address society as a whole but did not connect with many, including the Black and Asian communities. This is featured in a government report on tackling inequalities during the pandemic. On communication it concludes: 'Using a wider range of channels and approaches to communications were crucial to reaching audiences who might not always engage with traditional media. Tailoring content and partnering with specialist media helped to cut through and to land messages.'[2]

It is beneficial to find a way to hear directly from the communities affected to understand what is needed from the crisis communication. In developing these approaches communicators need to be aware of their own biases in delivering communication. Perhaps there are assumptions about the impact of media outlets, or that social media connects with all key groups. Ensure your crisis communication is rooted in evidence and research on communities, the impact of communication and issues that matter.

In addition to building a crisis response that is diverse and inclusive it is also essential to review the language that is used. Our language can easily be misunderstood, confused or in the worst case be offensive to people. Consider carefully the wording you are going to use and if possible test it on a diverse range of groups or individuals who can provide advice. This is something that can be developed as part of crisis preparedness and does not have to wait until a situation emerges. In the development of crisis plans assess the language you would seek to use and what impact it has, both positive and negative, and use the feedback to refine your plans.

As the crisis develops ensure your approach provides bespoke and not just blanket communication. Communication should become tailored to those affected, those interested and those involved at the earliest moment possible after the initial communication about an issue emerging. If you are working globally being aware of cultural differences, traditions and history is essential. Use your understanding, or that of a locally based adviser, to inform your content, approach and language. Where possible we need to approach communication by recognizing the individuals that are involved and the groups they may be connected to.

Understanding intersectionality is essential throughout the crisis communication activity, which is why understanding customers and stakeholders is vital. People cannot be characterized in simple groupings, as they may be impacted in a number of ways. For example, they could be in a disadvantaged group, live in a specific area or have a certain background, and all of these could overlap. This needs to be considered to ensure your communication approach becomes more sophisticated. There will be a whole range of communication channels and platforms that will have to be considered and having good links to them before an incident happens is important. Organizations should consider having diversity leads who work both within the business and also help to identify those key stakeholders and community leaders outside of the business. This will all be beneficial to the consequence management activity and crisis communication plan.

What is consequence management?

In Chapter 3 we outlined in some detail the issue of establishing consequence management to support the response. It will be part of the roles and responsibilities detailed in the crisis communication plan and has a key part to play in ensuring consistency across communication activity. While consequence management is very much associated with the crisis response from public agencies it can be introduced to all forms of crisis communication management. Public agencies use consequence management to ensure vital services continue and to manage and mitigate problems.

Consequence management does exactly what it says it will. It analyses the consequences of the crisis and the response in all forms, both intended and unintended, and then looks at how these things can be managed most effectively in the days, weeks and months to come.

The consequences are those ripples that appear on the water and being able to identify them and put mitigation in place is an important skill for the communicator. The focus must be on minimizing the detrimental impact of the crisis on stakeholders, customers, employees or the wider public. It may be that there has been a breakdown on the production line, which is the crisis. Consequence management would define who would be adversely affected by this incident, which may be delivery drivers, shops or franchisees, current customers, future customers, people living near the factory. The list could continue and as you can see, the key is to be open to looking at all possible groups or individuals that may be affected. In repairing the problem you may have another impact on those involved and this requires additional consideration. The system needs to be in place to be able to undertake this with the right people who can then support the business and communication in managing the crisis. It should build resilience within the organization, reduce negative impact from the events, identify key groups to support, identify opportunities for communication and manage any protest groups and individuals.

There are several ways that the consequence management element of the crisis response can operate, depending on the scale of the incident and the potential impact it could have. It can be run with key participants all sat together in a room near the crisis incident management room, or it can be run as a virtual meeting with people dialling in to a conference call. The approach taken will depend on the organization and the issue, but you should make it fit easily within the crisis management framework. Consequence management brings together representatives from the operational response, customer services, legal services and communication. Other roles can be added as required. It is a strand of the crisis plan and as such needs to have a named lead individual to oversee it and make key decisions. This must not be a communicator as they will be needed to deal with other areas of the response. In developing plans, you can train and establish a cohort of consequence management leads that can be called upon when an incident occurs.

A meeting of the consequence management group should take place quickly after the crisis has been identified so that it can start to report into the crisis management structures. It will assess the situation with the support of those involved in the group and will then produce a plan detailing the activities as the situation develops. The first key task for the group is to carry out the impact assessment so that the affected groups are identified. It may assist if this information is then plotted on a heat map showing where activity needs to be prioritized.

The communication team will ensure that the narrative and information that is provided about the situation is shared with the consequence management team who can then use it to develop further communication to critical groups. The communication contact sitting with the consequence management group will be able to review the communication to ensure consistency as well as identifying opportunities for proactive communication. Information needs to flow quickly and freely between the communication team and the consequence management team. This includes updates on the media and social media monitoring, mood evaluation and public confidence assessments, which can all support both areas of work.

Working with those affected and their families

In some crises there will be people who are so severely affected that they should be categorized as victims, and together with their friends and families they will be a critical group to the management of the incident or issue. The term 'victim' can be seen as negative and some people may be concerned about the impact of it as a label, so you may consider using the term 'affected people'. They are the people who in the most serious cases have been hurt, damaged, killed or have suffered because of the situation and possibly actions related to it. The impact needs to be assessed based on the circumstances but those affected could have suffered financial loss, loss of services, been inconvenienced or left isolated, or experienced psychological impact.

As we have said, the way we respond and support these people and their families will be one of the most important ways by which the crisis response will be judged. Talking about people as victims may

FIGURE 6.3   Example of a consequence management heat map

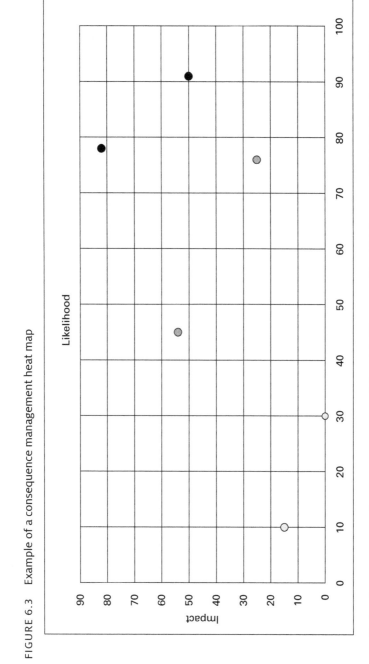

Each point represents an issue or consequence of the crisis. The ones with a high impact and high likelihood are red ●, high impact and low likelihood or low impact and high likelihood are amber ◐ and low on both scales are green ○

feel a little strong if the situation does not involve a criminal or terror-ist act but you can see them as the people most severely impacted by the situation. What you call them is irrelevant; it is how you recog-nize them and put actions in place to support them that matters. I will use the term victims to refer to those most significantly affected by the incident or issue.

The victims of a crisis could be the individual who faces illness because they have been caught up in a food contamination situation. They could be the people who have bought goods only to have been left waiting for them to be provided because of a delivery failure. They could be the people living in an area that is flooded or is left without electricity or other services. They could be those with a protected characteristic or part of a specific group that are reputa-tionally impacted by the situation. How you support them must be a central part of the response. Is the business being accountable for what has happened, and showing empathy and caring about what has happened? They should also be at the heart of the communica-tion approach and activity. Focusing on the impact on the business and its reputation will appear heartless and uncaring, leading to a negative view of the response. People are what matters in the crisis communication plan.

The business needs to have defined who will be best placed to support and liaise with the victims. It could be that you have specially trained individuals from a customer service background who have the required skills to support the victims. Alternatively, you may recognize individuals within the team who have the necessary abili-ties to perform the function effectively. Being a support to victims can be very challenging and will test the resilience of the employee. They should be given every support to undertake such a role, with training beforehand if possible and welfare checks throughout the time they are carrying out these duties. There will inevitably be a difficult situ-ation where legal departments may feel such support is an admission of guilt and responsibility for what has happened. However, this is not the case; it is about ensuring support is available and working with others such as Victim Support, the Citizen's Advice Bureau or other charities that may be able to assist those affected.

SKILLS REQUIRED TO SUPPORT VICTIMS

Those individuals who are chosen to work with victims in the aftermath of a crisis need the following skills and abilities:

- empathy
- resilience
- knowledge of business processes
- organizational understanding
- communication skills
- patience
- the ability to remain non-judgemental
- listening skills

Communicating with victims

Keeping the victims and their close families updated on the developments in managing the issue or incident is central to the liaison. The aim is to ensure there is never an occasion when they learn about what is happening through the media or social media. This is more ambitious than it may appear. With the speed of the delivery of communication, particularly through social media, information is out in the public arena instantly. We have all seen footage collected as a crisis incident develops that is instantly streamed online and shared immediately through social media platforms. It makes briefing and updating victims hugely challenging. In the initial stages you may not even know who the victims are so can only be sensitive to the fact that there are affected people you have not yet defined. In developing your messaging and narrative you can reference them even before they have been identified. Media statements can be started with an acknowledgement that it is a difficult time and support is in place for those affected before talking about other aspects.

Once they are identified it is essential to have a process by which you can provide those affected and their families with information and updates quickly and ensure that they understand what to expect from the liaison with the business. You could consider having a physical or virtual meeting with them within the first 36 hours of the crisis emerging. The meeting will be to explain what the business is doing to deal with the crisis and to manage the situation, to be clear about how the communication plan will work and when and how they will receive updates, and also to ensure they are aware of how the media will operate in broadcasting about the crisis.

It is important that communicators don't assume that people will all understand what they may face from media and social media when they are caught up in an incident. It is also essential that in providing information there is no attempt to sway the decision that the person makes about whether to speak to the media about their story or not. They should be given details of options alongside the positives and negatives of them all. The decision about whether to speak to the media, or to use social media to tell their story, is something they must make on their own and they should not be influenced by the business. The business should be able to recognize that the decision is made independently, and they must deal with the consequences of these actions. Any attempt to 'gag' affected people will be hugely damaging to the reputation of an organization and you should expect that in some way the detail of the actions will become public. In large-scale incidents victims will all approach the situation from their own personal circumstances so there will be some who want to talk to the media and others who want to avoid it. The organization must allow people the freedom to deal with the situation in their own way but be there to support as and when required.

TOP TIP

Have a small leaflet or flyer that explains about how the media operate within the base country of the business and abroad. Detail what it will mean for the affected person, such as that they will be contacted for comment, may be offered payment for an interview, and that if there has been a fatality the photographs and details of their loved one will become public quickly. Be sure that it includes details of where they can go to get advice or to make a complaint, for example any media regulation process that is in place in their country.

Principles for victim communication

There are eight key principles for how victim communication should be approached by the organization. These should be remembered throughout the management of the crisis and in every communication that is undertaken. Ensure those working on consequence management are aware of them and what they mean for any meetings, discussions or conversations they may have in the execution of their duties:

1 Open
2 Honest
3 Victim-focused
4 Supportive
5 Independent
6 Continuous
7 Attentive
8 Conscious of trigger points

Open

The communication should be shared without being unfairly or unnecessarily edited by the organization or the victim support role. People must be given the information in as much detail as possible so they can understand what has happened even if they can't know the 'why' it has happened until later. The affected people should not feel they have to keep pushing to get information from the business; it should be freely given. In the UK medical professionals work under a duty of candour, which is also being considered for wider application. The duty of candour guidance explains it as '… to ensure that providers are open and transparent with people who use services. It sets out some specific requirements providers must follow when things go wrong with care and treatment, including informing people about the incident, providing reasonable support, providing truthful information and an apology when things go wrong.'[3] This clearly has a significant impact on the crisis communication approach, the plan that is put in place, the messaging that is used and how transparent an organization is.

Honest

There should never be an occasion when the business does not tell the truth to those who have been severely and adversely affected. Being dishonest will irreparably damage the relationship with those affected and any trust in the organization will disappear. Honesty is always the best policy and if you can't provide the details explain that you can't and why you can't at this stage. Even if the information is something that may be controversial or upsetting it should be provided but with careful consideration of how it is given and what support may need to be in place for those affected.

Victim-focused

As we have stated throughout this chapter, the way the business deals with people will be important whether it is judged to have been effective in crisis management or not. Put the people affected at the heart of how you develop the communication. The best operational management of a crisis will always fail in the minds of the public if it has neglected to support the people most affected.

Supportive

The work with victims and families should always focus on how they can be supported, whether that is just listening to a problem or trying to make a connection to some form of support agency. It should not be a relationship that is based on directing them to undertake some action or activity. If the business finds this approach challenging then it may want to consider having advocates who can be there to connect the business to the affected people. They will be able to act to create a meaningful dialogue between the victims and the organization. Some affected people may quickly appoint legal representatives to undertake this role. If that is the case then they can and should be included in the process of updating and communicating with the affected people.

Independent

The relationship between the victim liaison and the organization should be a very loose connection. The individual undertaking the role should be impartial and operate neutrally. This can be one of the most challenging things, which is why involving another agency such as victim support charities may often be the best way forward. Any communication should be factual without value judgement so that the affected person can make their own decisions or form their own views about what has happened.

Continuous

If you are going to engage in communication with victims and victims' families then it is not a one-off activity. It cannot end once the initial communication and information has been shared. This is a continuous relationship that should be in place for some years to come so that any ongoing support or assistance can be identified and provided. The impact of a crisis can last for many months or even years, as we will see in Chapter 8 when we discuss the recovery phase. Building a strong relationship that will continue into the future will ensure maximum support is in place for those affected by the crisis and its aftermath. This does not stop when a crisis ends, particularly in significant situations that have fundamentally changed people's lives.

Attentive

Communication is often seen to be all about what is shared, talked about or broadcast. One of the most critical elements for effective communication is listening. It is also important for effective crisis communication to listen to the feedback about the crisis, what people are saying about the response and what is being said by employees. Listening to the views of victims and victims' families should be at the centre of the support and response. As we have said, understanding their views and issues can assist in adapting the response and developing the communication. Always ensure you are open to people's views and listen to what is being said.

Conscious of trigger points

The crisis will last for a finite period but the impact of it may roll on for many months or even years. Those people who have been adversely affected by the issue or incident will have to live with the impact of what has happened for the rest of their lives. It is important in the long-term relationship that is developed to anticipate times when things may be brought into focus and cause distress to the victims; such times may be anniversaries, the publication of reports or similar events happening somewhere else in the world.

Victims Commissioner

In the UK the Government has created a Victims Commissioner, who is an independent person appointed by ministers to advise, challenge and offer views that will promote the interests of victims and witnesses. The principles of the role were initially set down in the Domestic Violence, Crime and Victims Act 2004. While they don't have the remit to be able to champion individual cases, they can review services and make recommendations.

The Commissioner also has the role of monitoring compliance with the requirements set out in the Code of Practice for Victims of Crime. The Code is part of the Government's approach to making the criminal justice system focused on putting victims first. It establishes a minimum level of service that victims should receive and was created at the same time as the Commissioner role.[4]

A collective approach

In the planning and preparation for dealing with a crisis, being able to work with others and develop a collective approach is the most beneficial way forward. In Chapter 1 we discussed how it can improve and enhance the communication if it involves other key organizations or agencies. The same is true in developing the victim communication and working to support those who are affected. In the principles of victim communication, we outlined that having a clear and open approach to communication is critical. Those affected will have a lot to deal with and a lot to consider, so being able to streamline the number of agencies or organizations that make direct approaches will allow them breathing space to deal with what has happened. This means using the relationship that the business has developed to share updates and information from other key agencies as well. This also can benefit those affected who feel they have a single point of contact to use when they have questions or concerns that they need to raise.

Developing a collective approach does not mean limiting the access to information for everyone but it is about providing a structure and process that will be easy for the individual and their family to understand. When a person is caught up in a crisis it puts them into an alien position where they are not sure of what to do, what is happening and how to deal with what has happened. Providing them with ways to access support and to know how to ask questions or raise concerns is a critical part of the victim–business relationship. Helping and supporting the victims is a key part of the crisis management plan, which makes it a vital part of the crisis communication plan.

It is imperative to remember that a collective approach should ensure there are no gaps in the response and support to the people most severely affected. The relationship should identify additional help and support that is needed or information that needs to be provided now or in the future. If we think about a product failure, then it is important to be able to provide important health or safety advice to the affected person, update them about the work being done to recall and replace the item, and any compensation that may be available. If the business is being open and honest in its approach, then it will be comfortable in appointing someone to be the liaison point and help the affected person access all the relevant information regardless of the possible legal implications to the business. This may sound like a nirvana that many communicators may feel is out of reach of the business they are working with or supporting. However, it is the mark of a mature and developed business that it feels able to undertake this work without concern about any negative impact.

What is stakeholder management?

Stakeholder management is not the same as victim communication and support. The two should not be confused as they require different skills and approaches. Stakeholder management is also not the same as consequence management, which we discussed earlier in this chapter. However, the two are linked and do need to be closely aligned to have maximum impact. Stakeholder management is about developing engagement with the key individuals and groups, which we discussed earlier as part of the development of stakeholder mapping. The plan will need to have the full support of the CEO and top team as it will require them to undertake some of the key actions including briefing other senior leaders in key organizations. Understanding who the stakeholders are is the first stage but then the crisis communication plan must find a way of identifying how and when to converse and engage with them. Therefore, the development of a stakeholder management plan is important. It will be able to take account of the relationships that already exist in defining what communication activity needs to take place.

TOP TIP

Develop a stakeholder management plan as part of the consequence management activity. Detail in it who the stakeholders are, how frequently they need to be communicated with (use the mapping of interest and influence to assist in defining this, Figures 6.1 and 6.2), what channel of communication will be used and who will take responsibility for doing it. This will assist in ensuring that people know exactly what they are responsible for and can monitor that it is taking place as outlined.

CONSEQUENCE MANAGEMENT CHECKLIST

The following is a checklist of the key actions and activity required in the early stages of dealing with a crisis, and establishing a consequence management team:

1   Gather up and share the crisis communication plan.

2   Bring together key individuals from sections of the business, e.g. operations, customer service, communication.

3   Ensure a meeting is in place quickly to establish the framework for updates.

4   Discuss the situation using data and analysis.

5   Develop a stakeholder map.

6   Create an impact assessment specific to the crisis.

7   Ensure a lead is in place and responsible for consequence management.

8   Develop a stakeholder engagement plan that can sit alongside the crisis communication plan.

9   Be clear that the timescales for both the communication and stakeholder engagement match up.

10   Provide regular updates on developments to the person leading the crisis response.

11   Create a victim communication plan and ensure the people who will be making the connection are briefed and ready to be deployed.

12 Establish a timescale for the plans and situation to be reviewed, linking with any meetings to check the management of the crisis, and ensure key people are kept updated.

CASE STUDY
KFC

Early in 2018, KFC had a significant problem to deal with. During a change in the supply process they ended up without chicken at its restaurants. There was an outpouring of fury and concern on social media from customers who were frustrated by their failed attempts to get fried chicken. It even led to people contacting the police to complain about the situation.

KFC very quickly recognized a mistake had been made and there was a swift management apology for the situation. This was followed by an explanation of what it was doing to try to rectify the situation. It went on to take a lighthearted approach to the apology, taking out a full-page ad in the UK's national newspapers. The advert showed an empty KFC bucket with the initials changed to say 'FCK' alongside an apology for the restaurants being closed.

The advert had the following wording:

A chicken restaurant without any chicken. It's not ideal. Huge apologies to our customers, especially those who travelled out of their way to find we were closed. And endless thanks to our KFC team members and our franchise partners for working tirelessly to improve the situation. It's been a hell of a week, but we're making progress, and every day more and more fresh chicken is being delivered to our restaurants. Thank you for bearing with us.[5]

Saying sorry

In making a swift apology and from a very senior level in the organization, KFC demonstrated that it was aware and actively seeking to sort out the situation. But more than that, it went on to show that it had a good understanding of its customer base and what the organization's values are when it took a lighthearted approach, making fun of its position but not downgrading the seriousness for the franchises and employees. Using humour is always problematic but it worked well here because of the clear understanding of the organization and who it is talking to and working with daily.

KFC demonstrated it was being open, transparent and above all authentic in its response. Making an apology is always problematic because of the concerns raised by legal teams that it is an assumption of guilt. However, in this case the apology was carefully worded, and covered all those affected – customers, staff, franchise partners – which ensured that it had demonstrated an understanding of who would be adversely affected. It had also ensured that the employees were at the heart of their public response.[6]

All this work meant that the damage to the reputation of the organization was minimized and was hardly noticeable.[7]

Key learning points

- Ensure that you understand who your customers and service users are before any crisis may happen.
- Conduct stakeholder mapping and refresh it on a regular basis.
- When devising your crisis communication plan, develop scenarios with linked impact assessments that can be utilized when a crisis occurs.
- Actively demonstrate an understanding of who is impacted and what you are doing to help them.
- Consider when and how an apology may be required.
- Ensure there is a close relationship between developing the consequence management plan and liaison with stakeholders and the wider communication.

CASE STUDY
Kinder Egg product recall

In April 2022, shortly before Easter, chocolate-maker Ferrero recalled batches of Kinder Surprise eggs due to a potential outbreak of salmonella. An investigation was carried out by the UK Health Security Agency (UKHSA), Public Health Scotland, Public Health Wales and Public Health Agency Northern Ireland.

The recall was initially said to be a precautionary measure and restricted to the one product. But a few days later the recall was extended to all products from the factory in Belgium. By 8 April, 150 children in the UK and Europe had become ill, with some requiring hospital treatment.[8] The situation then spread to other countries including the US and Canada.

There were reports that salmonella had been detected at the Belgian site in mid-December 2021 and measures to address it were put in place.[9] In the April recall the company appeared to move quickly and to take pre-emptive steps to prevent problems. In a statement Ferrero said: 'This serious event goes to the core of what we stand for and we will take every step necessary to preserve the full trust and confidence of our consumers.'[10] Early reports included details that some of those affected were going to take legal action.

Within the statements provided there was a focus on what the company stood for but no details of what was being put in place to support those affected. The company website did not feature details of the recall and there was no social media communication. In addition there were no media interviews undertaken.

Key learning points

- There was an opportunity to address the problem in December when the issue first occurred, and this may have averted a full-scale crisis. Developing systems to gather data and information will assist in spotting anomalies and trends that may allow early detection of problems.

- Find people, don't wait for them to come to you. The social media absence impacted the ability to get information out to a broader audience. Consider where the people are who need the information and prioritize those channels.

- Effective crisis communication needs people to be at the centre of the strategy and that means ensuring there is appropriate support, prioritizing those affected within the communication and the response.

- Avoid being silenced by legal advice. Communication guidance is as relevant as it considers the impact on reputation and confidence in the business. Ensure legal and communication advice are considered together and discussed in detail. Even if the advice is to avoid providing comment there is always something that can be said in response to a crisis situation.

- Rebuilding reputation takes time and should not be rushed. It is important to recognize that the situation can impact on trust and confidence for a long time into the future. For some businesses and brands a severe crisis that is poorly managed can mean the end. Focus on acting appropriately and then working on rebuilding in the aftermath.

Conclusion

Communities are made up of people, and defining your community around the crisis will support the work to manage the consequences of what has happened. This is work that can, and should, be undertaken before any crisis happens. Understanding customers and service users is essential to the day-to-day communication activity. Alongside this, stakeholder mapping supports communication plans, not just at the time of a crisis. Working together with stakeholders can assist in the development of a consistent narrative.

Through the risk management process, make sure you have developed an impact analysis that looks at each possible risk and rates it on likelihood and expected impact. This will help to develop mitigation and to ensure that crisis communication has considered what may happen. Keep all these documents under review, particularly if the business' operating procedures or activities change.

Understand how consequence management works and what it means for the activity, structures and processes that are required. This element of the crisis response works hand in hand with communication so build a strategy that makes this clear. The consequences can be for the community as defined, or for the affected people. These people, who may be labelled as 'victims', need to have special care and attention within the crisis response. Remember, 'victim first' should be the approach for all communication. The affected people should be considered or communicated with before the media or social media.

Finally, work with those who have specialist knowledge and experience of supporting victims or affected people. Understand what they have to offer and how you may be able to access it. Work to meet the principles of victim communication throughout the crisis response, from the moment it is identified right through to the recovery phase. Always remember why you are doing it. It is not a checklist or tick-box exercise – it is about doing the right thing to support those most affected by the crisis.

Notes

1 B L Perry, B Aronson and B A Pescosolido. Pandemic precarity: Covid-19 is exposing and exacerbating inequalities in the American heartland, *PNAS*, 2021, 118 (8). www.pnas.org/doi/full/10.1073/pnas.2020685118 (archived at perma.cc/8E7V-EPXB)

2 Equality Hub and Race Disparity Unit. Final report on the progress to address Covid-19 health inequalities, GOV.UK, 3 December 2021. www.gov.uk/government/publications/final-report-on-progress-to-address-covid-19-health-inequalities/final-report-on-progress-to-address-covid-19-health-inequalities#communications (archived at perma.cc/N64V-4TD7)

3 Public Health England. Guidance: Duty of candour, GOV.UK, 5 October 2020. www.gov.uk/government/publications/nhs-screening-programmes-duty-of-candour/duty-of-candour (archived at perma.cc/9LH2-TXFT)

4 Victims Commissioner. Annual Report of the Victims' Commissioner 2018 to 2019, 1 July 2019. www.victimscommissioner.org.uk/annual-reports/annual-report-of-the-victims-commissioner-2018-to-2019/ (archived at perma.cc/52X4-E3R2)

5 R Priday. The inside story of the great KFC chicken shortage of 2018, *Wired*, 21 February 2018. www.wired.co.uk/article/kfc-chicken-crisis-shortage-supply-chain-logistics-experts (archived at perma.cc/AGN6-FH9Y)

6 A Hickman. The crisis comms lesson behind KFC's 'FCK bucket', *PR Week*, 8 November 2018. www.prweek.com/article/1498405/crisis-comms-lesson-behind-kfcs-fck-bucket (archived at perma.cc/CZC7-MY79)

7 A Topping. 'People have gone chicken crazy': what the KFC crisis means for the brand, *Guardian*, 24 February 2018. www.theguardian.com/business/2018/feb/24/people-have-gone-chicken-crazy-what-the-kfc-crisis-means-for-the-brand (archived at perma.cc/NC22-GTFT)

8 J Lee. 'He looked dead'. Mum's horror as son, three, hospitalized by 'salmonella from Kinder egg', *Express*, 15 April 2022. www.express.co.uk/news/uk/1596653/kinder-eggs-health-news-salmonella-hospital-wales (archived at perma.cc/LD4W-HBAQ)

9 J Whitworth. Ferrero passes probation at salmonella-hit factory, *Food Safety News*, 17 September 2022. www.foodsafetynews.com/2022/09/ferrero-passes-probation-at-salmonella-hit-factory/ (archived at perma.cc/QRQ7-6UEV)

10 C Schofield. Kinder recall: which batches of chocolate has Ferrero pulled from UK supermarkets after salmonella outbreak? *National World*, 10 May 2022. www.nationalworld.com/health/kinder-recall-ferrero-salmonella-uk-supermarkets-3639478 (archived at perma.cc/NKV3-FYMU)

7

It's OK to not be OK:
Ensuring support is in place

A crisis will hit individuals in many ways, including physically, emotionally and psychologically. Dealing with these aspects is something that should be recognized and covered in all organizational crisis plans and emergency planning, as well as being reflected in the crisis communication plan. As we will see in this chapter, the recognition of the impact, the support to employee wellbeing and the importance of managing the damage at all levels is vital to any crisis. It may be argued that the role of developing a resilient organization and ensuring wellbeing is at the heart of the crisis response are not issues for the communicator. However, as we identified earlier, the professional communication lead can be the ideal person to act as a catalyst in developing the response, planning for the inevitable crisis and providing an emotional barometer when a crisis occurs. Communication teams, alongside any customer service representatives, will be the ones at the forefront of making connections with customers and service users. They hear information first-hand, can analyse the impact of the situation and provide emotional awareness that can be fed back into the nerve centre looking at the response. Communicators are therefore the ideal people within the business to promote the idea of support and wellbeing during a crisis and other significant events and developments.

Organizations have a duty of care to their employees and that means taking all reasonable steps to ensure their health, safety and wellbeing. This is more than a legal duty; there is an ethical requirement and looking after staff directly impacts on productivity at work. Remembering wellbeing is always critical to the business. This is why it requires the roles of wellbeing coordinator and wellbeing communicator to be directly linked to, and involved in, the crisis communication plan. Creating this plan and testing it is often overlooked in favour of assessing the initial response phase. However, as we outlined in Chapter 4, the way people are supported by the organization when a crisis happens will be a critical factor in judging whether it is felt to have been effective. If your existing crisis response plan and associated policies don't include a consideration of wellbeing, then it is definitely time to update them. People have a huge amount of sympathy for the employees of businesses that are caught up in a crisis and the support available will come up in the questions from the media.

Recognizing the impact

The scale of the impact of events on people's psychological and emotional wellbeing will depend on many factors, including the details of the crisis, the history of the business and the personal circumstances of the employees. It is impossible to chart all the people affected by a crisis individually from one central point in the organization unless you have a very small team running the business. This makes it essential for managers and senior leaders within the organization to be trained on how to identify those people who may be suffering or in distress before, during and after a crisis. They are not expected to be experts in the field, but they are expected to be able to provide regular updates on the number of people affected and the range of support that is required. These managers provide the early warnings of who may struggle and who appears to be starting to struggle so that they can be given support as soon as possible.

If we remember the analogy of the stone making ripples on the water, then the impact of the crisis will affect people in very acute ways if they are at the centre of the ripple where the stone has entered the water, and the impact will lessen the further out we go. Those at the centre of dealing with a crisis may be affected by post-traumatic stress disorder (PTSD), requiring one-to-one counselling, help and support from trained specialists. Those further away from the centre of the issue may be affected but in a lesser way that will need talking therapy or some form of group counselling. However, things do not always follow in this very simplistic way. You could have an employee showing signs of PTSD but on the fringes of dealing with the crisis. This is why being able to recognize the signs that people are struggling, and being able to signpost people to support, is critical.

People can show signs of PTSD immediately after a traumatic, stressful or distressing event or it can appear many months or even years later. It has a tremendous impact on the person's life, as they will relive events and may have problems sleeping or concentrating.

It is estimated by the NHS in the UK that PTSD affects one in every three people who have had a traumatic experience. The key is to recognize the signs of it as early as possible.[1] People caught up in difficult situations can suffer mild symptoms of anxiety and stress, but it is when these feelings last more than four weeks that it becomes important to check with your doctor. The key for managers is to be aware that PTSD is a possibility for those caught up in a crisis and while they are not expected to be able to diagnose, they must be able to spot someone struggling and ensure they are directed towards the right medical support. If they don't recognize the signs then the person may require a significant time away from work to recover, which affects the operation of the business.

Employers should consider the psychological and emotional impact of work on their employees. This will ensure that they are ready to deal with these issues when caused by the impact of a crisis. If they fail to consider wellbeing then they are likely to have staff off sick, will see others leave the organization or see work performance dropping as people struggle to concentrate. All these things can affect the bottom line of the business' performance so if the business doesn't accept the moral responsibility then bosses may see an impact on profitability. The central thread is ensuring people are resilient to the challenges that may lie ahead. This has to be developed over time and cannot be introduced at the moment a crisis hits. A resilient workforce will be able to keep calm, develop the crisis response and be able to weather the storm.

Modern pressures

Modern life and difficult situations can lead people to suffer from stress, anxiety and depression. The statistics show that the number of people who have experienced one of these conditions at some point in their lives is incredibly high, alongside high suicide rates. The World Health Organization estimates that one person dies every 40 seconds worldwide due to suicide.[2] This is the case for people dealing with the pressures of modern life, all before they may be caught up in, or have to deal with, a crisis. Dealing with a crisis can be the final straw for some people already struggling to manage issues in their lives. Businesses must be able to recognize those who may be struggling and at risk should they be caught up in a crisis. The key is always to ensure the appropriate support is available at the earliest opportunity.

Welfare and wellbeing are an ongoing responsibility for employers, and are not something that can be ignored. However, as with crisis communication planning, wellbeing support can be seen as a 'nice to have if we have time'. Taking this approach will be storing up problems that will emerge at some point in the future. Failing to look at the welfare of staff will ultimately have an impact on the recruitment and retention of employees. This means that welfare is not just an issue for the days and weeks when the crisis is underway, or for the months ahead and any trigger points. It is something that must be part of the healthy organization and should be considered as part of the business objectives and measures.

Creating a resilient organization

The importance of a plan for wellbeing within the business cannot be overemphasized. It is a critical element to support employee engagement and to ensure the retention of the most talented people to work within the business. Creating a resilient organization is something that must be part of the culture and built into the policies, processes and procedures. No business should wait until a crisis hits to consider the wellbeing and resilience of employees. Building resilience takes time but it can be improved by ensuring there is a strong risk management focus within the business and encouraging everyone to be involved in the crisis management training and exercises. If people understand what will happen and the role they have to play within the management of a crisis at all levels, and not just in the communication management, then they are more likely to be able to cope when they are put under pressure because of an issue or incident. Keep an eye out for people who show signs of stress during the testing process. People who do can be given extra support and training to ensure they are more able to deal with a crisis when it happens, or you may decide to alter the responsibilities that people have, to minimize the pressure on them.

For communicators, being resilient and appearing calm under the pressure of dealing with a fast-paced crisis is essential. Emotional awareness should be part of the training plan in any continuous professional development that they undertake. It is important for them to be aware of their own emotional response and how they can manage it to ensure they are able to keep a level head to deal with the crisis. However, they must also be able to spot the signs of stress and pressure on those around them. Training for employees looking at resilience, managing stress and keeping themselves well can be value for money, bringing financial benefits to the business. Remember, if there is funding available, bringing specialists in to assist with this training will be more cost-effective.

Communicators themselves have a central role in managing any crisis so they will be a key group requiring monitoring and consideration as to whether psychological and emotional support is needed both during and after the crisis. It is worth remembering that it is not just the crisis that can push people to breaking point. They may have dealt with a series of really challenging or upsetting issues at work that when put in close succession test their resilience. Again, being able to spot the signs of someone who is struggling with the pressure of ongoing problems is also important. Consider who has knowledge of which staff may have been involved in difficult or challenging projects, and what do they do with that information. There will undoubtedly be more that they and the organization could do with that information to put greater support in place.

Creating resilient communities

Governments are continually looking for ways to ensure individuals and communities are ready to respond to the most serious crises. There are ongoing programmes to ensure people know what to do if they are caught up in flooding, wildfires and terrorist attacks. Government-developed national campaigns run to ensure people understand their role and what they should be doing both to prepare for an emergency and to respond when one happens. The explanation of the plans helps people to be clear what will happen, where to go to for help or assistance and how they are expected to behave, for example, evacuating the area. The more involved communities are in planning for national and local crises the more likely they are to be resilient when something happens. They can understand more about what is happening, what they can do to help manage the situation and how developments in the situation may impact on them. At the heart of this work should be an attempt to ensure they are alert to emergencies that may happen but also that they are not unnecessarily worried about them. For example, those living in areas of flood risk should know what signs and warnings to look for, how to protect themselves and reduce the impact on their property, and how to access help. If they know where to go and how to respond they will work more effectively with emergency responders.

Businesses do not need to develop such large-scale crisis communication campaigns, but they can start conversations with customers and service users to explain their planning and training. For example, if you are a food manufacturer you can find ways to proactively explain how you will communicate about any contamination or product failure issues. This should be part of the work to show the business takes safety incredibly seriously and is working hard to avoid problems but is also preparing in case something happens. If you go back to the scenarios that you have outlined within the crisis communication plan then you can consider whether there are any communities, groups or individuals that you could start to have discussions with about the crisis response. The training and planning for a crisis should never consider only the actions required within the organization; they need to look at how the plans can be shared with stakeholders and other key groups. Preparing and getting people to think about the possibility of a crisis will start to build resilience. They will understand what could happen and what they can do to help with the situation. For example, if you are a bank customer you need to understand that cyberattacks can happen and if you recognize a fraud situation you need to know where to report it and how to protect yourself.

There are four key points to building a resilient community:

1 Have a clear plan about how those affected will be supported; this will support the 'victim' plan.

2 Discuss the support that is available, from medical services to those offered through mental health charities.

3 Prepare a timeline to consider the trigger points and how to mitigate their impact (more about this later in the chapter).

4 Don't lose sight of the human impact of the crisis and that this will continue for some time after the incident has happened.

Wellbeing before a crisis

Organizations should have some services and employee wellbeing programmes in place as part of the daily business. Even the smallest business needs to know how it will deal with wellbeing issues. It is important to be aware of what is in place, what is covered and how quickly support systems can be put in place should a crisis emerge. Organizations must ensure they have access to psychological and physical support services and that this information is built into the crisis plan. To have to find support and to try to understand where to go when a crisis has occurred will cause unacceptable delays to developing support for those affected. If the issue causes a significant impact to individuals or communities, as we discussed in Chapter 6, then consider how those affected can be supported and where assistance can be found. There are many charities and organizations that exist to support people affected by a whole range of issues and they may be able to work with the business to manage the impact of what has happened.

TOP TIP

Understand what psychological support is available and can be accessed both by employees and those affected by the crisis. It may be through health services, health providers or through charities and third-sector organizations. Contact them in your area or nationally to ensure you know where to go, the helpline numbers to share and how to get in touch at short notice.

The planning and preparation to deal with a crisis must refer to putting a welfare lead in place to ensure the business is supporting the staff that are adversely affected. This role will work closely with the internal communication lead to ensure that staff are told about how to seek help and support if they feel they are struggling to deal with what has happened. The welfare lead also needs to work with the human resources or personnel section of the business to ensure consistency of the support that is available. This is often an aspect of the crisis preparation and planning that is neglected and so once the process has been written and communicated it should be subjected to some form of testing. The test will look at whether the individuals undertaking that role can step up quickly to become the welfare lead, will assess how the role works with other sections of the crisis management response and will review the assistance that can be made available.

The consequence management work can ensure that those who are adversely affected by the incident are identified so communication activity and support can be put in place. In addition, the work to provide support to 'victims' will also help in devising wellbeing and resilience support that may be required for communities and individuals. In short, the work to plan and prepare for a crisis must always consider the welfare and support that is required and what should be put in place very quickly.

Wellbeing during a crisis

Below is a checklist to assist in the immediate response to a crisis to ensure that welfare and wellbeing support is being considered and put in place.

1 Use the consequence management work and impact assessment to help identify those who are adversely affected by the issue or incident.

2 Identify the employees who may be most severely affected.

3 Ensure the initial internal communication provides details of where to access help and support if employees feel they are struggling to deal with what has happened.

4 Put a meeting in place with consequence management, internal communication and human resources to coordinate activity.

5 Provide regular updates to staff about how to access support services.

6 Ensure managers are aware of how to identify staff who may be struggling and know how to signpost them to find help.

7 Develop a plan of visits to key departments and teams within the organization who are at the centre of managing the crisis. The aim is to ensure senior leaders, or the CEO, can visit to boost morale and ensure wellbeing is being considered.

8 Consider what support network is in place, or should be put in place, for people who are affected to mirror the employee wellbeing that is available. Note that in a national emergency criticism can follow when

victims and victims' families feel they are not given emotional and psychological support, but the emergency responders have access to a range of such support.

9 Identify what external support is available for the public who may be affected and reference this within media work, as well as circulating details through social media.

Wellbeing in recovery

In the next chapter we will discuss in detail the issue of recovery and when and how the organization should move from dealing with the crisis to moving into recovery. One aspect of the recovery will be to ensure there is ongoing support to those who have been adversely affected by events. This support needs to continue even when the cameras have gone and the media interest has disappeared. Dealing with the emotional and psychological impact will take months or even years. In some cases, people will be in denial that there is any problem until there is a trigger that unlocks pent-up emotions.

Communicators must be aware of the ongoing challenge from the aftermath of the crisis and the sensitivities required in the recovery phase. There needs to be ongoing support that remains available once the rush of the crisis has died down. In all the internal communication that takes place in the weeks and months that follow the crisis there should always be a reminder of how employees can access help if they need it. This may include a helpline, drop-in facility or online portal to access help. Plan for the wellbeing support and communication activity to continue for months and keep it under review alongside the decisions around the recovery phase, which we will discuss in the next chapter.

Another simple way of improving morale and boosting wellbeing across the workforce is to find a way to recognize the hard work and commitment that people demonstrated during the crisis. It won't take away from the trauma people have faced but it will provide a positive opportunity to reward people for the effort they have put in.

Recognition is an important way to provide a boost to employees. It can be as simple as just meeting people and saying thank you, which we covered in Chapter 5 when we looked at leadership. If the crisis is significant and means people are doing some difficult and challenging work, then it could be beneficial to develop a more formal recognition process. This may be in the form of an event, some token of appreciation or a bonus payment. However, the organization must always consider how this may be viewed by those who are 'victims' of the incident or issue. It can appear insensitive to be 'celebrating' in some way once the crisis is over because many people may still be dealing with the impact it has had on their lives. For example, consider if you are a bank that has suffered a significant outage. Many people may have lost money or been penalized because they could not pay bills. The bank has agreed to cover these costs where people can evidence the negative impact. Managers at the bank realize that some key employees in IT and customer service have worked excessive hours and gone above what was expected, and they want to reward this effort in some way. In providing staff with some form of bonus or reward it may be seen negatively by people still working to get their costs reimbursed. Be sensitive in finding ways to recognize the effort of employees.

The crisis will continue through to recovery and into the future. It is essential that a timeline is developed that will assess and review the potential trigger points that could impact on people's wellbeing. It is important to recognize the impact of anniversaries and other factors that can require wellbeing interventions. This timeline should be used for both internal and external communication activity as the triggers will be similar. It will guide you towards the work that may be required in the future to continue to be sensitive to, and support, people's recovery.

Finally, all the learning and experience gathered in dealing with the crisis and the aftermath should be captured. Organizational wellbeing programmes and welfare support should learn from the experiences and be improved and developed from the feedback. This should be included in reviews and a part of the debrief process that has already been outlined. Debrief the wellbeing and welfare support that was in place during the crisis with key members of the organization as well as other support agencies and stakeholders. Keep data on the kinds of issues and problems that arose and the support that was required. You can use information about the issues and any problems to develop and enhance the wellbeing support that is provided. If you are aware of what support was required it may signify where resilience training can be focused to help develop employees. Gather as much data as possible in relation to the wellbeing support required during and after the crisis. Be clear about what trigger points emerged during the crisis. During the debrief ask what worked, what didn't work and what could be done differently in future. All this data, insight and information can significantly improve any wellbeing programme that is already in place for employees. It is data that will also assist in the review and development of the crisis communication plan. There may have been gaps in the approach, a lack of resources focused on the wellbeing and internal communication aspects, or lack of management buy-in to the work that needed to be actioned; the strategy and plan should be updated to ensure this is improved when managing future critical issues or crises.

What are trigger points?

We have mentioned a few times during this chapter the issue of trigger points but what are they? Put simply, the trigger points are times or events when the crisis is brought back into the spotlight not just of the media, but of employees or the wider community. The timeline document will chart all the potential triggers so that the situation can be tracked, and relevant communication activity put in place to mitigate the impact. The following are all possible trigger points for those adversely affected by a crisis:

- key dates such as one week on, one month on, six months on and a year on from the crisis;
- publication of any reviews or debriefs;
- inquiries, investigations and inquests, all of which will have specific dates;

- a similar crisis or issue happening somewhere else in the world;
- a similar crisis or issue happening within the business;
- the early warning that a similar crisis may be on the horizon;
- other situations that may be vicariously linked to the issue or incident;
- publication of any statistics that will include information linked to the event, for example details of annual food contamination figures after a similar crisis.

This is not an exhaustive list and you may find there are additional trigger points when dealing with your crisis. When you look at the scenarios you have outlined and the issues raised in your risk management matrix you can consider what trigger points might exist. This will help you develop the thinking process required when you are working on a timeline for a live issue or incident. Developing the details of the trigger points and working through the future impact will give clarity on the timeline document. This can then lead to the crisis communication plan being updated ready for the move to recovery and beyond.

FIGURE 7.1   Example of a trigger points plan detailing known events and announcements that may have an impact on affected people

Month	
March	• Report published • National figures released
April	• Revision to production line • Announcement about product changes
May	• Share announcement • Board meeting
June	• New building opens in location • Public meeting
July	• First anniversary • Local events/meetings

Communication and wellbeing

The communication team are not the people who should lead on the wellbeing strategy or the organization. The work should be under the remit of either a wellbeing coordinator or sit within human resources, organizational development or another such central function. Communicators will already be stretched to undertake the work that is required to manage the crisis communication, so the skills and expertise of others should be put in charge of the wellbeing response. The wellbeing work is essential to support people and continue to improve the public view of how the human impact is being managed. The CEO and senior team should be aware of this work and find ways to be able to support it daily. This is a key element of the leadership role and demonstrating care and support for the workforce and affected people outside of the organization.

The communicator's role within wellbeing is to provide support by making people aware of the help that is available and by replaying back to the business how the response is being viewed. They can provide data to give insight into the impact and people's views on the success of the response. Communicators need to have the confidence to challenge the wellbeing response provided by the organization and how people are supported. If the team works in-house this can be difficult to do, which is why bringing in external support to assist during and after the crisis may be beneficial. But they will be the best team positioned to have an early alert to where gaps may exist, as those staff are very likely to have complained to the media or using their own social media accounts. The communication team should know their channels in detail, and not only know how best to share the information about the wellbeing support that is available, but also be able to monitor channels and identify areas of concern.

The communication team should push for the wellbeing aspects to be part of any exercise that is undertaken to test the crisis plan. It may seem like an area outside their remit but as they will have responsibility for developing an internal communication plan and understanding the affected people and what is required they will be focused on support in a way that other departments will not. They can prompt the business to include the wellbeing response in the training and exercising linked to their communication plan. Doing this will provide valuable data about how to develop the plan and identify where problems may exist. It also helps to put the issue of wellbeing and welfare onto the table for the managers involved in the exercise. The more these issues are discussed, talked about and included in the planning process the more likely it will be that they will be accepted as part of the crisis response. Communicators can facilitate that happening when working through both internal communication and community impact work.

CASE STUDY
Pakistan International Airlines crash

On 22 May 2020, flight 8303 on a domestic flight from Lahore to Karachi in Pakistan crashed as it was preparing to land. The Pakistan International Airlines (PIA) aeroplane crashed into a busy residential area of Karachi. The impact killed 89 passengers and eight crew on the flight, and also eight people on the ground. Only two people on the flight survived the crash. The pilot had aborted an attempt to land the plane and issued a Mayday call just before the flight crashed.

Immediately there was speculation about the cause of the crash, including damage to the plane caused by the aborted landing, and pilot error. An initial report by the Pakistan Civil Aviation Authority blamed pilot error for the aborted landing and then damage to the plane that was not identified.[3] It was the third plane crash in five years involving PIA flights.[4] In the aftermath of the crash Arshad Malik, the CEO of PIA, issued a statement while boarding a flight, which was viewed as a casual response. Even before the investigation had concluded, the CEO appeared to suggest he could not understand the pilot's actions.[5]

It was some hours after the accident before a statement appeared on the PIA Facebook page and the first statement on the PIA Twitter account was on 28 May.[6] The website finally had an emergency contact number and message of condolence but no other information and no rolling updates on the situation. In the aftermath, families of the victims of the crash had complained about the lack of information and cooperation from PIA.

One family member posted a number of concerns and criticism about how the situation had been handled. This included failing to support the search for his family, who had been on the flight. In one video clip, Arif Iqbal Farooqi said he was 'tired of going from one hospital to another' visiting mortuaries and police sta-tions in an attempt to trace his family. He said bereaved families were being sub-jected to red tape and that 'the federal government, the Sindh government, PIA officials and administration had left them alone'.[7] Families were frustrated with a lack of coordination at a time of intense grief, which could lead to a long-term impact and effect on them. People expected that PIA would have appropriate plans and support that would be put in place in the event of a plane crash.

Key learning points

- Those who are at the centre of a crisis, including families who have been bereaved, should be at the centre of the crisis response and the communication. Support mechanisms should be put in place to provide them with all the help they need to navigate through the situation. This means communication about where to go and how to find information.

- Plans for key risks and potential crises should be in place, tested and ready to use at a moment's notice. This requires careful consideration of how to provide support to those affected but also to support those involved in the response, who may have to deal with the most horrific circumstances.

- Leadership is an essential part of an effective people-focused crisis response. Strong leadership that demonstrates empathy and compassion, while also implementing the systems that are needed to help those most affected, must be in place.

- Information should be provided quickly, accurately and consistently in the days that follow the emergence of the crisis. Families who have lost loved ones should know where to go and how to receive regular updates. This can go some way to helping them at the most difficult and traumatic time in their lives.

- Give those affected by the crisis a way to ask questions, to understand what has happened and listen to any concerns that they have about the response. Engagement is essential, as without these opportunities affected people will use the media and social media to voice concerns and even anger about the response.

- Avoid speculation, particularly when a formal investigation is underway. The focus should be to provide those affected with accurate information and support that allows them to grieve. Speculation adds confusion and can lead to concerns about the accuracy of the information that is being provided.

Conclusion

Managing a crisis requires empathy and it is vital to remember all the ways the situation has, or can have, an impact on people. This includes understanding the psychological, emotional and physical impact of what has happened. Ensure that this includes looking at the impact on all affected people and communities, as well as employees. Build wellbeing into your employee communication plans, because you can't develop it in the aftermath of a crisis if you have not considered it as part of daily operational business.

People can respond to a crisis in many ways and this includes experiencing post-traumatic stress disorder (PTSD). You don't have to try to understand the implications alone; there are many charities and voluntary organizations that work with mental health issues and will be able to provide assistance. Before a crisis happens, make sure you know what is available to support employees and focus on developing a resilient organization. This means ensuring a robust risk management process and providing appropriate training for managers to be able to support their teams.

Resilience is also something that can be created from the wider environment around the business. Starting conversations and discussing with customers about how crisis management will happen can ensure that they are more prepared should the worst happen. If they understand where to go for information and what they need to do then they are more likely to feel an element of control over the situation. This is about being alert but not alarmed by possible events. Wellbeing support and assistance is required throughout the crisis but also into the recovery phase.

Communicators should be able to assist the business in understanding the trigger points for the future; the points in time and events that may put pressure on people psychologically and emotionally. If you are aware of when and where these will, or may, occur then you can put appropriate support in place.

Finally, recognize the good work, dedication and commitment of the employees who have responded to the crisis. It is one way of demonstrating support for them and should be part of the wellbeing plans. But be careful how this recognition and any form of reward will be viewed by those affected by the situation, otherwise you may face another reputational crisis. Remember to also recognize the efforts of those who have kept the organization functioning when a crisis occurs. They may not be in the middle of events but play a key role in managing regular business, which allows others to dedicate time to managing the crisis.

Notes

1   NHS. Overview – post-traumatic stress disorder (PTSD), last updated 13 May 2022. www.nhs.uk/conditions/post-traumatic-stress-disorder-ptsd/ (archived at perma.cc/5FKF-LBL8)

2   World Health Organization. Mental health – suicide data, 17 June 2021. www.who.int/news-room/fact-sheets/detail/suicide (archived at perma.cc/K6QP-HCPX)

3   BBC News Asia. Pakistan plane crash was 'human error' initial report, 24 June 2020. www.bbc.co.uk/news/world-asia-53162627 (archived at https://perma.cc/6EPD-ESMD)

4   Dawn.com. A timeline of major air crashes in Pakistan, *Dawn*, 22 May 2020. www.dawn.com/news/1558945 (archived at perma.cc/M253-FMUC)

5   Express Tribune. PIA Air Chief Marshal Arshad Malik gives official statement regarding the PIA aircraft crash [Facebook] 22 May 2020. www.facebook.com/watch/?v=246141083275453 (archived at perma.cc/3HTQ-NNX9)

6   @Official_PIA [Twitter] 22 May 2020

7   K Hussain. Red tape adds to agonies of crash victims kin, *The Express Tribune*, 27 May 2020. www.tribune.com.pk/story/2229412/red-tape-adds-agonies-crash-victim-kin (archived at perma.cc/RWE4-6XK9)

8

Stepping on the road to recovery

The road to recovery following a crisis can be a long and difficult one. It is one of the most important aspects of the crisis response and can make the difference between moving forward positively or suffering long-term reputational damage. Think about when you have suffered from some illness or a bout of flu; you don't suddenly feel back to normal and able to do everything you used to do. It takes time to recover and you need to look after yourself. The same is true of the crisis recovery. You need to work on it and accept that it is going to take some time to move forward.

Recovering after a crisis is made easier if you have had a successful response to the initial issue and the early stages of dealing with things. Communication that has been developed in the way we have discussed throughout this book will put you in a good position to deal with the response. If you have implemented the key elements, then you should be able to move forward positively. If not, then the recovery phase may be your last opportunity to turn things around and develop an effective response.

As with all the work on the crisis communication plan, you must ensure you have considered what is required regarding communication in the recovery phase. Understanding what recovery means and what it will look like will assist in the development and refinement of the crisis communication plan.

What is recovery?

Recovery is a time when you have managed the initial impact of the crisis and are moving forward. It is when you are dealing with the long-term aftermath of the crisis, looking at the learning to take forward, mitigating the issues to guard against any future recurrence of the problem and rebuilding reputation. Later in this chapter we will talk about the issue of reputation and where it should feature in the work to recover after an incident or issue has run its course. Failing to consider and plan for the long-term impact of the crisis has the potential to be costly to the business both financially and reputationally. This planning has to consider all the elements of the response including the communication. When you start to look at the communication issues around recovery it is important to know where you want to get to or get back to. Look at what is important to the business; what does it want to achieve and what does the plan look like for the next five or ten years? Keep that end goal in sight even though recovery may take many months or years to complete.

Making the move from crisis response to recovery is not easy and choosing the right time to do it is essential. Crises can run for some time and maintaining the communication approach and refreshing it during a situation that can last for years is a huge challenge. In such cases the move from crisis into recovery could be many months or even years away. The decision requires careful consideration and discussion with all the relevant parties involved in the response. This can include the operational staff, the HR staff, communication lead, consequence management lead and those supporting the affected people. It may also need to involve other key agencies, particularly when they are stakeholders or are part of the response. There are both physical and emotional factors to take account of when considering moving forward and away from the crisis phase. Physically you will see a reduction in the number of staff involved in the response and any central control room or 'war room' will become audibly quieter with fewer people working within it. But alongside this there are emotional factors involved. The affected people dealing with the impact of what has happened may impact on whether a decision is made to move to recovery. For example, if you have suffered a product failure then the problem may have been identified and rectified but if people are still falling ill or being affected then you would be criticized for talking about moving to a recovery phase. As with many elements of crisis communication management it is people who hold the key to an effective recovery, including when it starts.

Long-running crises

In some situations a crisis can last for an extended period of time, although this is not common. There is an assumption that a crisis may last for a day or a week or possibly even a month and, until the Covid-19 pandemic, a crisis lasting more than a year was thought unlikely. When managing a long-running crisis communication plan there are a number of factors to consider. It requires a change in mindset at the point it is identified that it will last for some time. In such situations, there will be a requirement to resume the usual business operation while still managing the actions needed in response to the crisis.

Patience, determination and resilience are three critical factors when managing the communication of a long-running crisis, or if the organization becomes known as being crisis-hit because of a series of issues. Communicators like to problem solve and get things done but with a crisis over an extended period of time this will take longer to achieve. Being able to recognize the small steps to take on the road through the crisis without attempting to rush ahead is essential. This may be a frustrating time but communication can only go at the speed of the crisis itself. Being resilient and able to continue to drive communication through a serious crisis or a number of crises is the most important element. For those working closely with a business or organization, such moments can feel like a personal attack and as if there will be no way out of the difficult position. Crises do have a lifespan and the five stages mentioned in Chapter 1 will always play out, even if it happens over years rather than days. In Chapter 7 the importance of building resilience was outlined and long-running situations will be a huge test of any communication team. Ensuring they can maintain some perspective on what has happened, find time to switch off, and know where they can get support will assist in building resilience.

With any long-running situation it is important to keep focused on it and to ensure it is part of day-to-day considerations. The balance will need to be found between undertaking 'normal' activities and delivering crisis communication support. When communicators feel fatigued it is important to take some time away to recharge and return refreshed and ready to continue the work.

There are six key elements to remember when managing a long-running crisis:

1 **Strategy** – during a long-running situation the strategy will change, develop and be refined. The approach should be reviewed at regular intervals, assessing what has changed, whether the communication so far has worked, how the problem may develop and what has been learnt from the crisis so far. Update the strategy and ensure that those providing the crisis communication response are aware of what the strategy is and how it has changed from the one they may have been working to deliver.

2 **Evaluation** – this is a critical element of any crisis communication activity and must not be overlooked. At key points during the long-running situation, carry out an evaluation assessing the effectiveness of the communication and ensure it covers outputs, outcomes, outtakes and the impact on the organization. If something is not working then look at an alternative course of activity and refine the approach being taken.

3 **Consultation** – understanding what people think and feel about the crisis as it develops over many months is a vital part of the strategy and evaluation. Finding ways to listen to external voices will assist in developing inclusive and effective crisis communication.

4 **Focus** – it is easy to lose the focus needed on a problem when it carries on over a long period of time. Build the management of the issue into your day-to-day communication tasking processes

and monitor the activity as you consider work that is underway. During a long-running crisis, communication has to be sensitive to undertaking work that may have a negative impact on the crisis, and particularly on those being affected by it. For example, an organization promoting a change to a product that may be at the centre of a crisis will be seen as insensitive, leading to an additional reputational crisis.

5 **Mood** – monitoring the mood that exists around the crisis is critical. If you become focused on the internal issues and how the crisis is affecting the business without considering others, it will be seen as 'tone deaf'. The steps should be taken at a pace that is acceptable to those affected by the crisis and to the wider society. Track the mood around the crisis, as the situation may change over time.

6 **Creativity** – throughout a crisis it becomes more challenging to find ways to continue to connect with people to ensure they understand what is happening and what it may mean to them and to the business. The same problem can exist within an organization as staff become fatigued with an ongoing crisis. A long-running crisis gives the communicator the opportunity to be creative and find ways to continue to develop the conversation and to engage.

In addition, it is essential to consider the resources that are required for long-term crisis communication. Extra support may be required, either to boost the team or to have a person responsible for managing the ongoing crisis issues. For example, if you have had a situation emerge that leads to a public inquiry it may keep the organization in crisis communication mode. In such cases, an additional communicator may be recruited to focus on just the public inquiry and any ongoing issues. If there is no possibility of securing extra resources then careful prioritization of the workload is necessary. Crisis communication requires significant staffing and resourcing to achieve and cannot just be added to the workload of an existing team without stopping other projects or activities.

There is also the requirement to ensure continuity for any long-running situation. Senior managers and even the CEO may change a number of times during a crisis that continues for years. For example, in the UK the Post Office prosecuted hundreds of sub-postmasters and mistresses when money went missing but it was subsequently found to be due to a failing computer system. This issue began in 2000 and it was only in 2022 that convictions were quashed and a public inquiry was launched.[1] The crisis has developed over two decades and during this time senior managers will have left the business, so understanding exactly what happened will be an additional challenge. Ensure that when dealing with any crisis situation information is logged, reported and captured for both the ongoing situation and any future re-emergence. It will also assist in learning the lessons about what happened, why it happened and how things may need to change in the future.

When new employees join the organization they also need to understand the situation surrounding the crisis. This can be done by finding ways to introduce it into any induction programmes and having clear communication to ensure the business can continue to function. A long-running crisis does not have to derail an organization if there is a plan in place and it is understood by employees. Communicators can learn to live with an ongoing crisis that is part of the working day if there is a clear strategy, systems and resources in place throughout.

Making the decision

There are several elements that must be considered before the CEO or Gold Commander makes the decision that the organization is ready to move to recovery. However, there is no simple formula to decide when recovery should happen, as every crisis is unique and involves unique factors.

The questions that need to be asked include:

1 What stage is the response at?
2 Are people still coming forward to say they have been directly adversely affected by the crisis?

3 Is the crisis under control and not growing or expanding?

4 Is the business able to return to usual operational activity?

5 Is the number of staff involved in the response being scaled back?

6 Are people starting to think about the future rather than dealing with the present?

7 What is the public mood towards the issue or incident?

There may be other important questions that need to be asked and the communication staff can consider what these may be based on the details of the crisis. For example, if you have suffered a data breach that has left customers vulnerable you will need to be comfortable that the full extent of the problem and implications are understood and have been managed before even considering moving forward. There will be technical details that can help define at what stage recovery can begin. So as you move away from the immediate response to the emerging crisis through towards its conclusion, start to consider what factors would signal the move to recovery.

If we look at each of these questions in turn it may help to understand the mindset and thinking that needs to be in place to consider the future and when to declare the organization is in recovery mode.

What stage is the response at?

A simple question to gauge what has been done and what activity is still required. If the bulk of the original plan, and communication plan, has been achieved then it may be an indicator you are moving into a new phase and that is likely to be recovery. However, if there are still a lot of outstanding actions then you may need to delay a move to recovery and focus more on the continued operational response.

Are people still coming forward to say they have been directly adversely affected by the crisis?

If you have identified all those most severely affected and have appropriate support in place, then that is a good indicator you may be able to move forward. However, if there are still elements that are unknown or not yet fully identified and these may mean that new 'victims' could come forward then you are definitely not ready to start to consider stepping into the recovery phase. It is worth noting here that even if you are taking the first steps in the recovery phase you can halt it and move back to the crisis response if it is required. The situation can fluctuate, which is why it is important to recognize you are in pre-recovery rather than the full recovery phase of the crisis. This may happen when new groups of affected people come forward. But this can weaken the crisis response so it is more advantageous to delay the decision to move to recovery rather than push ahead.

Is the crisis under control and not growing or expanding?

This may seem like a very simple question, but it is often problematic to identify whether the initial situation has stagnated or is continuing to develop. Work closely with colleagues leading the operational response to ensure a clear understanding of what has happened, what is happening and what may happen in the future. If it is felt that the crisis has levelled out and is not continuing to spread or grow, then it may be an indicator that you can start to consider the recovery phase. As mentioned before, don't be in a rush to push ahead with recovery, as having to step backwards can be potentially damaging to an organization's reputation. Instead, be cautious and delay the move to recovery if the situation may still deteriorate or expand, and keep the situation under review.

Is the business able to return to usual operational activity?

The day-to-day business will have been affected during the crisis. Resources will have been diverted to manage the response and this can impact on normal activities. The crisis may have had only a minor impact on the operation of the organization, or it could have severely impeded the production of items or the provision of services, but either way it will mean the usual operation has been curtailed. If the business is starting to operate as it would have done before the crisis, with the same output ratios, sales figures and investment opportunities, then it may be time to start discussing the move to recovery. Again, if there are still significant resources assigned to the crisis response then you are unlikely to be ready to move to recovery.

Is the number of staff involved in the response being scaled back?

The number of staff working on the crisis and involved in the response will fluctuate throughout the issue or incident. If you were to chart it the figures would start low, as people are made aware of the situation and are starting to implement the crisis plans.

FIGURE 8.1   Example of staffing levels during the lifetime of a crisis

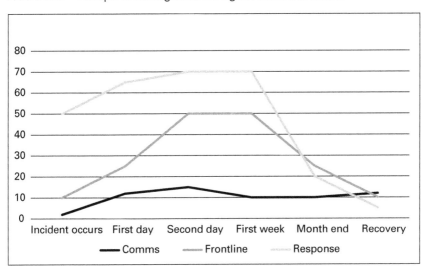

It would then grow to the high point when the bulk of the operational response and activity is required. And then, as the actions of the crisis plan are completed, fewer members of staff will be needed to work on the issue. It is often only the CEO and the communication team who are the last people to be working on the crisis while other employees go back to 'normal working'. If the number of employees involved in the crisis is starting to reduce and the response scaled back, then a discussion on stepping into recovery may be required. Don't be in a rush to move to recovery, as you may find the situation changes and staff are reassigned back to the crisis response. The reduction in staff needs to be sustained over a significant period of time. What that significant period is very much depends on how long the crisis has been underway.

Are people starting to think about the future rather than dealing with the present?

If the business and its departments are starting to think about how they can build for the future, then you may be moving towards recovery. When people are dealing with the crisis they are very firmly fixed in the present situation and cannot look up from where they are to start to consider what will come next. It is the difference between living day to day and being able to focus on a three- or five-year plan. If discussions about the longer-term future of the organization are starting to appear in the daily business, then you may be ready to discuss the move to recovery. But remember that this cannot be taken as a factor on its own as people may be rushing to move on to get some distance between themselves and the crisis. You must consider this as just one indicator.

What is the public mood towards the issue or incident?

This is a key indicator of when to be able to move from crisis to recovery. If those affected and the people around them are still dealing with the impact of what has happened, or if the scale of it was so serious that they are reliving the events that took place, then you are not ready to start to move to recovery. If an organization starts to move forward too quickly then they may be accused of being insensitive and failing to understand the impact of what has happened. This was seen with BP and Tony Hayward during the Deepwater Horizon disaster mentioned in Chapter 5. Being sensitive to the public conversation and tone about the issue or incident is important as it will mean you are aware of the prevailing view and will be able to operate from a position of knowledge. As we have mentioned earlier, having monitoring in place is critical throughout the lifespan of a crisis. This monitoring and feedback from your affected people and stakeholders will support the consideration of when may be appropriate to move to recovery.

Even when you may have been able to answer all these questions positively and from a position of knowledge, you could still decide to allow more time before declaring a move to recovery. There is no simple formula, but it would be beneficial to use any community links and key stakeholders to gauge their views on the time when moving forward may be appropriate. It will also be important to discuss this with whoever has been the face and voice of the business throughout the crisis. They will need to be comfortable that it is the right time to help the organization move on. If they get it wrong then you will find there is an additional demand on the crisis communication response as you have to repair the damage from appearing to dismiss the situation and move forward.

Training for recovery

Once the initial crisis is under control the interest from those within the business about what has happened can significantly wane. Employees will be returning to normal activities. This can leave the organization struggling to keep a focus on effectively managing the crisis through into recovery. It may also mean the communicators are the only people still heavily focused on dealing with what has happened. A vital way to overcome this is to create a recovery phase of the crisis response plans that is tested in exercises and training. A recovery communication plan should develop from the crisis and this plan can be tested in the same way the initial response to a crisis is exercised. Start by reviewing the plans and what they mean for the final phase of the crisis. Ensure that the crisis plans the business operates under run from the first alert right through to re-establishing normality.

If there is a test or exercise being organized, then build in questions to test the understanding of the recovery phase. If time allows for it then arrange a separate training session or exercise just to discuss the decision-making process around the move to recovery and to check the systems are in place to continue to effectively manage the situation. For example, who will make the decision, how they will decide, what information should be provided to allow them to make an informed decision. Don't lose public confidence in the business by failing to plan for the recovery phase. Again, if you are unable to run this test using staff from within the business then consider bringing in some expert help and advice to stress test the plans. This includes the crisis communication plan that must be tested. For example, you may find that the number of communication staff working on the issue needs to increase in the recovery phase. This can only be ascertained if you have put the proposed plans for recovery phase working to the test.

All those involved in the response phase need to understand what recovery will look and feel like. What are the key aspects of the scenarios that you have outlined in the planning phase? Looking at these will help point to how the crisis may be concluded. What will need to have happened before the situation is seen to be under control or being effectively managed? Consider each scenario during your planning. For example, with an IT failure you will know that systems will have to be up and running again and you must have a clear understanding of who has been affected and how before you can consider pushing into a recovery phase. It is important to understand the nuances and the small signs that point towards recovery and not just rely on a feeling that normal business has been resumed. Investing time in the development of plans to think beyond the initial response is essential to effective crisis management.

The focus of recovery

There are three key elements that are the focus of the recovery phase of crisis communication: reputation, trust and confidence. All three will be central to the communication activity that is undertaken once the crisis has been brought under some form of control. Reputation must never be the sole aim of crisis communication because it will mean poor decisions are made based purely on what is best to protect the name of the business. During a crisis, decisions should be made based on what is best for those who have been adversely impacted as this will be one of the most significant factors that determines how the business' response will be judged. Remember the details in Chapter 6 looking at the support for victims and those affected. Reputation is built positively when the organization shows empathy and genuine concern for the people involved. However, when you are considering the elements of recovery communication then rebuilding the reputation of the business needs to be part of the aim. Part of it, but not the whole focus.

Trust and confidence are the key building blocks to encourage people to view an organization's reputation positively. People need to feel that the communication that has taken place throughout the crisis has been honest, trustworthy and authentic. If any element of trust has been lost or tested throughout the crisis then ensure you have identified it and can then look at how it can be rebuilt in the aftermath of the issue or incident. People, whether customers or service users, must have confidence in the business both in dealing with the crisis and being able to move on from it. This is as well as feeling confident in the authenticity of the communication. All this is built through effectively implementing the elements of the crisis communication response that we have discussed up to this point. However, if you have been unsuccessful in part of the communication the situation is not lost. The key is to take all the learning throughout the crisis and ensure you can build a strong recovery communication plan.

TOP TIP

It is advisable to develop a recovery communication plan that will take forward the work that has been underway during the crisis communication phase. Use the recovery communication plan to consider what elements undertaken during the crisis need to be continued, what can be ended and what new work needs to be in place. Use any data and insight from the crisis to assist in developing the plan and build in a link to the organization's business plan and communication strategy.

When there is no return to normal

It is important to recognize that 'return to normal' is an unlikely situation when dealing with a significant crisis. Whatever the situation that has happened, or the crisis that you may have been dealing with, sometimes it will be forever linked with the business. This situation is also more likely to occur since the arrival of social media, meaning every issue leaves a digital footprint. It is important to be able to use the information and learning from the crisis to redefine and re-establish the business objectives and plans for the organization. We will review this in the case study later in this chapter.

What matters for those who have been dealing with the situation is that they need to be comfortable in defining a new normal for the business. Understanding and working through this can help people who have been psychologically or emotionally impacted by the events that have taken place. They will be able to see the events change the business for the better.

In some cases, the scale of the crisis is so vast that it will change the way society, or some parts of society, operate. For example, the terror attacks in the United States on 11 September 2001 were so unbelievable that they changed many aspects of society forever. There were new ways of working for air travel, new considerations around politics and foreign policies, and a changed view of how the world was. While that crisis was on a scale no one had ever anticipated, you can see the same need to revise the way organizations work and operate after every crisis. If the business is not looking at what can be learnt from the situation then it cannot build trust and confidence or ultimately rebuild reputation. It can also expect to see the same issues happening again as was seen with the case study of the Canadian Government departments cyber crisis in Chapter 2. Imagine you are a small business that provides financial advice and you have a data breach. You will have to make fundamental changes to the way you store and manage data in the aftermath of this crisis and this will become the new normal. Failing to make these changes will significantly impact on the reputation of the business.

The four Rs of long-term recovery

The long-term recovery of the business requires four elements to be in place: reviewing, rebuilding, resources and re-establishing. Each of the elements is essential to building strong communication to move the business forward after a crisis.

Review

Using the data, insight and monitoring that have been in place during the active phase of the crisis, assess what has worked, where any gaps are and what the reputation of the business currently is. It may be worthwhile utilizing some form of reputation tracker to assess against competitors and recognize the position. All this information will be essential for you to then create a long-term communication plan to identify the activity that needs to be in place in recovery. You need to understand what the impact has been to be able to focus the activity needed going forward.

FIGURE 8.2   A reputation data tracker working across the business sector

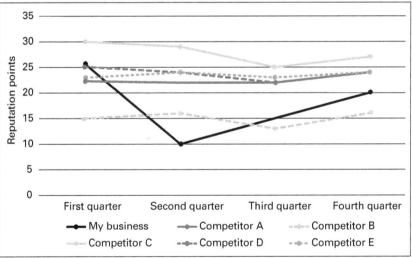

Rebuild

The data from the review section will provide the information needed to focus the plan to rebuild. However, you also need to assess any previous problems that have occurred, any outstanding issues or other factors that may impact on reputation. For example, the CEO may be under the spotlight for some unconnected issue, but this needs to be understood when you are devising the recovery communication plan. Be clear what the organization needs to overcome and what it needs to be recognized for when customers or service users are thinking about it. Is this still the same even after the crisis? Does the business need to do some work on the values, principles or priorities in light of what has happened?

Resources

One of the most challenging situations for a communicator leading a team in dealing with a crisis and then continuing through to managing the aftermath is the impact on resources. As we have discussed earlier, crisis communication demands a speedy response, which needs people to be trained and ready. Some of the staffing required may come from other areas of the business or from outside of the business if you have used contractors. The use of all these people will be finite due to the requirements of the sections that they may have been taken from or because of the impact on the budget if they are being brought in from agencies. The communication team is likely to end up in a position where they are simultaneously dealing with the aftermath of the crisis, looking at the recovery phase and needing to be returning to usual communication activity, and all this will have to be done with the same number of staff in place as before the crisis occurred. Assess the communication staffing levels required and prepare details of the number of additional staff that may be required in the coming weeks and months. Alongside the staffing you may want to request funding for a reputation tracking system if that does not already exist, as this will assist in the understanding of the impact of activity on rebuilding reputation.

Re-establish

The focus of recovery communication should be on re-establishing the brand, organization or company. This will require close working with the CEO and senior management team to support a review of the business objectives, policies and procedures to ensure issues identified from the crisis are considered. Review the organization's communication strategy to retain what is required and enhance it based on the learning and experience. This also needs the input of stakeholders who will be able to act as critical friends and offer advice about the way forward. If you have established victim support, then it is advisable to involve them in the future development of the business if at all possible. More developed and evolved businesses may be able to find a way to involve customers or service users at this stage as well. The key is to re-establish the business within society and ensure it is not isolated or marginalized due to the crisis. But be careful not to see re-establishing the business as purely a reputation management issue because that will lead to surface changes but no substance. It means that moving forward will lack a solid basis.

Debriefs and reviews

In Chapter 1, when we were outlining the work that was required ahead of any crisis, there was a significant focus placed on learning and training. This is the same at the conclusion of a crisis to ensure that you take the maximum amount from the experience. As a business you must be clear that you have mitigated any risks of the situation reoccurring in the future, and this should be done through a structured debriefing system. There are two stages to debriefing a situation. The first is done within a week or so of the incident concluding and should look at what worked well, what could be improved and any feedback that was received. Each area or department involved in the response should undertake this, and it can then inform a formal debrief.

The second stage is more detailed. It is recommended to bring in a facilitator to run a formal debrief event either for a day or a half day, involving the main leaders responsible for the response. Choose someone who has previous experience of undertaking this sort of facilitation role to ensure you get the most you can from the investment of time. This debrief will be a detailed look at the themes that may have come out in each of the quick debriefs that have taken place, and will identify what activity and work should be undertaken post-crisis and recovery. Any urgent actions should be noted and implemented as quickly as possible. It is possible to undertake this work while recovery is still underway, but it should not be carried out too quickly following the conclusion of the crisis phase of the incident or issue. The aim of the work is to ensure the crisis plans, including the crisis communication plan and the consequence management plan, are all updated with the learning from the response. This will refine and improve the plans for the future.

Once all the debrief work has been undertaken there may be a requirement to run a review to track the progress of any actions that have been identified. The public, affected individuals, stakeholders or shareholders may all want to know this information, to see that lessons have been learnt and to see the development of the business. Remember though to avoid the use of the phrase 'we have learnt the lessons' or similar in your communication as it has become overused and lacks any real meaning. It has no authenticity or honesty.

The debrief work and checking on the progress of actions post-incident could be linked to the existing risk management process that is in place but may be run separately and reported to the CEO or senior management team member. The crisis will have been a realistic test of the existing plans and there are always aspects that can be improved and learning to be gathered. Ensure you dedicate time and resources to gathering the learning and ensuring that you can strengthen the business processes, risk management and crisis preparations. The crisis will have been a significant challenge to the organization, and managing it, working towards recovery and rebuilding for the future brings extensive learning opportunities. Don't feel that the need to review and develop the crisis communication response is a signal that there was anything wrong or flawed with the action that was taken. It is merely a way of ensuring that you can improve and develop further.

CASE STUDY
Alton Towers

On 2 June 2015, there was an accident on The Smiler rollercoaster at the Alton Towers theme park in Staffordshire, UK. A train on the rollercoaster collided with a stationary, empty train, leaving 11 people needing medical treatment with five seriously injured. The most serious injuries led to two people requiring partial leg amputations in the weeks after the collision.

The response from the CEO of Merlin, who are the owners of Alton Towers, was swift and decisive. Media interviews were undertaken quickly and the company gave an apology as well as focusing on sympathy for the victims, with a recognition that the incident was ongoing, and speculation was to be avoided. A decision to close the theme park was taken quickly while the investigation was carried out. The ride itself wasn't reopened until March 2016, some 10 months later.

At the time of the incident, as well as providing interviews, the company website had its home page changed and its Facebook page was also updated to provide information in a timely way. The company also avoided any attempt to fight against a health and safety prosecution and moved to provide a settlement to the victims.[2]

Learning

The approach was clear and decisive, which showed it was in control of the situation and working with emergency services when the incident happened. The CEO at the time, Nick Varney, was visible in all the media interviews and always maintained a focus on the victims.[3] His comments focused on the sympathy for those who had been affected rather than any reputational issues for the company.

In one media interview, when asked about the effect on the share price of the company, he made it clear that it was not focused on that in the aftermath of the incident. A crisis of this nature, size and scale was always going to take some time to recover from. Alton Towers' management appeared to realize that it would need to accept a short-term financial and reputational impact but that with careful management and appropriate decision making it could recover. Figures appear to show that from a visitor number of 2.58 million in 2014 the numbers reduced to below 2 million during 2015 and 2016. By 2018 they had increased to 2.1 million, showing a move back towards the pre-incident attendance figures.[4]

Key learning points

- Follow the guidance in the previous chapters of this book: focus on victims, put a structure in place, act quickly and be visible.

- Remember that recovery time will vary depending on the nature and scale of the crisis so don't rush things.

- Take time before visibly moving forward; in the case of Alton Towers, reopening the theme park had to be done with sensitivity.

- To secure the long-term future of the business you may need to accept a short-term impact on profit or share prices.

- Be clear about the priorities for the future based on an acceptance of the business' position post-incident.

CASE STUDY
Peloton face financial challenges

During the 2020 Covid-19 pandemic and its restrictions on groups meeting in public, the exercise equipment company Peloton benefitted – it experienced a 440 per cent increase in sales, as people started exercising in their own homes instead of going to the gym.

However, that dropped by 76 per cent in 2021 as people started returning to their previous exercise regimes, and Peloton's sales in the first quarter were at their lowest in terms of growth, at 161,000 new users.[5]

In early 2022, a series of reputational issues put the business in the news headlines for even less positive reasons. A character in the Showtime TV programme *Billions* was shown suffering a heart attack while using the company's equipment. This came just a month after a similar scene in the programme *And Just Like That*. The similarity of the scenes was said to be a coincidence.[6] Ahead of the *Billions* screening Peloton tweeted that it had not given permission for the IP or equipment to be used. This was followed by an attempt to focus on the health benefits of exercise.[7]

There were then plans to reduce or halt the production of equipment, which were revealed following a leaked internal presentation from then CEO John Foley.[8]

Other claims surfaced at the same time saying the Tread+ would not be produced in the 2022 fiscal year, and that there would be job losses and closure of showrooms. An additional charge of $250 for delivery and set up of the equipment was introduced, a cost that had previously been included in the price.[9]

By the quarter ending in August 2022 the company had losses of $1.2 billion and there was a series of changes announced in an attempt to cut costs.[10] The focus was on cost-cutting, redundancies and outsourcing of production and delivery to realign the budget. There was also an agreement to start selling the equipment through Amazon in the US. It was a move away from selling only through Peloton's own website and showrooms.[11] Peloton was one of the companies that benefitted during the Covid-19 crisis only to struggle once restrictions had been eased.[12]

Key learning points

- Be prepared for crises to grow and develop or for more problems to occur that put the business under pressure. Communication strategies need to take account of all the issues that are being faced, those that occurr from within the business as well as those caused by unrelated external factors such as TV programmes.

- Avoid using language that is confusing or is difficult to understand. Business language is fine for business publications but when speaking to customers it needs to be easy to understand. Take care with the language that you use and check it is appropriate for the audience being addressed.

- Communicate changes clearly and in context. The business changes that Peloton was making should have been clearly explained, as part of a proactive communication strategy. There needs to be a defined narrative about the progress and development of the business. This can help to build trust and confidence in the approach and management.

- Bring marketing, PR and crisis communication together in the long-term development of communication. Peloton could have looked for other product placement opportunities that would challenge those depicted in the programmes mentioned. Identifying opportunities for the future marketing of Peloton should be part of a long-term crisis and then recovery communication strategy. Even if a business is not struggling commercially the perception that it is can be easily created and this can happen at any point in the future. Long-term plans are essential to rebuild confidence for a strong recovery.

Conclusion

Dealing with the crisis is the first priority but when the situation is under control it can signal a move to the recovery phase. Don't rush into this phase as it can take some time to feel able to move forward. Deciding when to move to recovery is key and it requires careful thought and discussion. Above all remember the affected people and the emotional impact of the crisis and its aftermath.

Training needs to be in place for all aspects of the crisis management plan and this includes dealing with the recovery. This is an area that is often neglected in favour of preparing for the first hours of the crisis but it must happen. Ensure the training and exercise plans include a focus on deciding when to move to recovery and what that actually means for the business. The recovery phase can be more complex and demanding than any other point during the crisis. A long-running crisis can put a significant amount of pressure on the communication and the team responsible for it. Such situations require more innovation, engagement and creativity as the focus continues over many months or years.

Reputation, trust and confidence are central to recovery communication. If you have implemented an effective crisis communication plan in the initial stages you can build on this through the recovery phase. Consider developing the strategy so that you have a crisis recovery communication plan. However, if things have not gone well for any reason, you can still turn things around if you have invested in understanding the elements of the recovery.

Be prepared that in some cases the situation that has arrived and challenged the business can fundamentally change the way it operates. It may be necessary to redesign parts of the business or to develop its operation. This is not something to fear, as, approached in a positive way, it can strengthen the business.

Finally, remember the four aspects of the recovery phase: review, rebuild, resources and re-establish. All these can keep the focus on what is required for the final phase of the crisis communication strategy. After that it is about debriefing and learning, and that is a sign of a healthy organization that is building for the future.

Notes

1 K Peachey. Post Office scandal: What the Horizon saga is all about, BBC News Business, 22 March 2022. www.bbc.co.uk/news/business-56718036 (archived at perma.cc/L8XC-AP5F)

2 A Monaghan. Alton Towers visitor numbers still down since Smiler crash, *Guardian*, 29 September 2016. www.theguardian.com/business/2016/sep/29/merlin-entertainments-alton-towers-visitor-numbers-still-down-smiler-crash (archived at perma.cc/K83F-W5S9)

3 J Harrington. Merlin CEO Nick Varney fronts response to Alton Towers crash, *PR Week*, 4 June 2015. www.prweek.com/article/1350007/merlin-ceo-nick-varney-fronts-response-alton-towers-crash (archived at perma.cc/TZ8N-L39N)

4 Themed Entertainment Association (TEA) and The Economics Practice at AECOM. Global Attractions Attendance Report, 2018. www.aecom.com/wp-content/uploads/2019/05/Theme-Index-2018-4.pdf (archived at perma.cc/AGW6-K36M)

5 B Stieglitz. More bad PR for Peloton! Billions character 'Wags' suffers heart attack after spin class in Season 6 premiere – following death of Mr. Big in Sex and City reboot, *Mail Online*, 24 January 2022. www.dailymail.co.uk/news/article-10433761/Pelotons-brand-gets-slammed-unfavorable-portrayal-Showtimes-Billions.html (archived at perma.cc/JA67-N4YF)

6 J Jacobs. Another Peloton Heart Attack on TV? 'Billions' says it's a coincidence, *New York Times*, 21 January 2022. www.nytimes.com/2022/01/21/arts/television/billions-peloton-premiere.html (archived at perma.cc/3URF-N9HB)

7 S Hamedy. 'A 'Billions' character had a heart attack post-Peloton ride. Peloton is not happy about it, NBC News, 24 January 2022. www.nbcnews.com/pop-culture/tv/billions-character-heart-attack-post-peloton-ride-rcna13296 (archived at perma.cc/RA37-HA99)

8 L Thomas. Peloton to pause production of its Bikes, treadmills as demand wanes, CNBC, 20 January 2022. www.cnbc.com/2022/01/20/peloton-to-pause-production-of-its-bikes-treadmills-as-demand-wanes.html (archived at perma.cc/BX2R-SQ5T)

9 J Valinsky. Peloton is hiking prices because of inflation, CNN Business, 18 January 2022. www.edition.cnn.com/2022/01/18/business/peloton-price-increase-inflation/index.html (archived at perma.cc/X6DA-MUT4)

10 *The Guardian*. Peloton shares plummet after quarterly losses top $1.2bn, 25 August 2022. www.theguardian.com/business/2022/aug/25/peloton-losses-shares-plummet (archived at perma.cc/5CS6-25TG)

11 T Ryan. Peloton looks to get back in shape by selling on Amazon, Retail Wire, 1 September 2022. www.retailwire.com/discussion/peloton-looks-to-get-back-in-shape-by-selling-on-amazon/ (archived at perma.cc/CU5D-LJQ3)

12 R Vlastelica. Peloton and Zoom show more pain for Covid trade, Bloomberg UK, 29 August 2022. www.bloomberg.com/news/articles/2022-08-29/peloton-and-zoom-show-covid-trade-can-t-find-a-floor-tech-watch (archived at perma.cc/L6YX-MY8D)

9

So, what happens next?

Dealing with a crisis can be daunting and you can put it to the back of your mind in the hope it may never happen. Hopefully, it won't ever happen but if it does you need to be ready and able to respond to it. As a professional communicator it must be part of your skills and knowledge to be able to cope with a crisis and as a business leader it is your responsibility to ensure the organization is ready to respond across all sections. Getting ready now will put you in the best position possible to be able to spot a crisis before it happens, respond quickly when it is underway and bring the organization safely through it.

The key to managing a crisis is to have done the preparation work and to deal with it in bite-sized chunks. If you attempt to implement the whole of this book single-handedly in one go you are unlikely to succeed. Take it a step at a time to build a successful crisis communication response. Develop a roadmap that will track your progress to ensuring you are crisis ready. This roadmap should be something for the whole of the business and not just the communication team. However, communicators can play a key role in developing the road-map and tracking the progress. Implementing a crisis management approach into the culture of the business takes time. Taking things a step at a time and really embedding the attitude and behaviour into the culture will achieve the best results. This is an investment of time to build a stronger, more resilient business.

There has been a lot of discussion about processes, plans and procedures for dealing with a crisis and they are all important. In fact, they are vital to ensure your readiness for the possibility of a critical situation that may develop into a full-blown crisis. But what is more important than all those things to the success of the response is to deal appropriately, sensitively and professionally with the people who are caught up in the crisis. It doesn't matter whether they are the employees who have had to respond to the situation or the people who were the most affected, how the business treats them will be a significant factor in the perceived success of managing the crisis.

Traditional approaches to crisis communication have focused too heavily on processes and reputation at the expense of the people affected. Strategies are written from the sole perspective of protecting the organization when they should look outwards and start from the perspective of the people caught up in the crisis. They should focus on gathering a diversity of thoughts and using inclusive language. This can be seen in many of the crisis situations and some of the case studies that are outlined in this book. We should never lose sight of the fact that all communication is fundamentally about people and a conversation, and crisis communication is no different. People are the recipients of the communication and they will also be caught up in the crisis. Changing the way you consider crisis communication and its aims will build a more effective strategy and approach. Consider what crisis communication means to you, your communication colleagues, senior leaders and the organization as a whole. If you understand what their views and opinions are before an issue emerges then you will know how much work is required to change the perspective away from reputation management and towards a people-centred response.

Throughout this book there have been key learning points, top tips and examples of how to prepare, manage and recover from a crisis. If you are struggling for time to develop your crisis communication strategy and plans, then just try to take some of the main elements from the points within this book and put them in place. The key is to have some form of outline in place even if you haven't been able to develop a fully formed plan. But I would recommend ensuring you have the strategy in place as soon as you possibly can. Ask for the time and support needed to write or revise the plan and to detail what is required to ensure readiness.

When you put this book down, make sure that you start to review what needs to be in place wherever you work or whoever you work for. A crisis could emerge tonight or tomorrow or in a couple of days' time and you need to be ready. There are no second chances in the world of crisis communication. Of course, if you want to have more peace of mind then make sure you have planned and prepared, including testing your plans. There is more on maintaining readiness later in this chapter.

The five Ps of crisis communication

There are five Ps to remember in developing your crisis communication strategy:

- People
- Plan
- Prepare
- Process
- Purpose

People

Remembering the people affected by the crisis is the most important element to take your crisis communication from being just enough to being effective. Most crisis plans and systems are developed without considering the requirements of the employees who are delivering the practical response, and the people caught up in the crisis. Customers, service users and, in the most serious cases, victims and affected people and their families, should be at the heart of the response. Remembering the people involved in the crisis will be fundamental to how people view and assess the business' response. Considering the needs of people cannot be underestimated; it is beneficial to the people involved and to the whole business.

Building employees into the communication response is also essential. They should not learn about the situation from anywhere but the company they work for. Getting internal communication right is as important as, if not more important than, any external media work. Ensure you have considered how the internal communication response will work alongside the external communication activity, particularly when considering narrative, key messages and timings. Any failure to communicate internally could easily be played out on social media, with staff and their friends and families commenting on the situation. Remembering to communicate with internal staff will also help when considering the wellbeing support that is required. Consider the welfare and wellbeing support the business has access to and identify how it can be used to help those who may be affected by what they have to deal with.

Mental health and wellbeing within communication and PR is much written about. It is recognized that PR is a stressful profession for people working in it day after day, and this pressure will increase during a crisis. This has to be acknowledged, and support built in, not just for those staff dealing directly with the crisis but for those who may be indirectly involved but affected. Communicators will learn more about the implications of the crisis than many other departments. They must have a clear picture of what has happened to inform communication and that can mean being aware of complex, difficult or upsetting information. The phrase 'It is OK to not be OK' is often used, and that is the case, but we don't have to accept that people will suffer without help and support. Build a wellbeing approach that can be tailored to individual affected staff, teams and the wider organization when needed.

For many years crisis responses have been delivered to people without a thought for the impact on those who are affected – the victims, as we have called them. If we look at the response from the CEO after the Alton Towers accident mentioned in Chapter 8, then we can see the importance of the humanity of the response. It doesn't matter whether it is an operational or reputational crisis, the way people are supported will be in the spotlight. Don't just prioritize it because it will lead to a more effective response – do it because it is the right thing to do morally and ethically. Showing you care about those caught up in the crisis, without accepting any liability for the situation, is important. Authenticity remains essential in all aspects of the people elements of the response. It is about more than following a formula; it is about being genuine and understanding the views of those caught up in the situation. This is why crisis communication plans and activities should be tailored to the organization. An 'off the shelf' crisis communication plan will not be as effective.

Finally, the people who are stakeholders or who are identified within the consequence management activity and any impact assessment must also be considered. Remember the ripple effect and the importance of working out who to contact, with what and when. Identify who is most affected and then work outwards, being careful to cover all those caught up in the incident. Be aware of the diversity of people and what this may mean to the communication approach. Detail how they will be updated and who will update them. Ensure there are open lines of communication between them and the business throughout the incident and into recovery. This will help manage the impact and ensure consistency in messaging. This may sound resource intensive but, as outlined in Chapter 6, there is a lot of preparatory work that can be undertaken as part of planning for a crisis.

Working to support the people affected by a crisis is not something that will stop when the initial situation is resolved. It will continue right through to the recovery phase and then beyond at all those trigger points mentioned in Chapter 8. You will need to consider the people affected by what has happened today, tomorrow and for some time to come. In the cases of organizations such as BP and Alton Towers they will always need to be aware of the key dates and issues that will bring the events they had to deal with back into the spotlight.

Plan

Having the right plan in place is critical; it needs to be developed so it is bespoke to the organization. It is the foundation for all the communication work that will follow, however long that is going to take to complete. All organizations are different and have their own issues, culture and background, and while you can learn from others you must make sure that it fits the business. It must have the business in mind and be linked to the existing risk management system. As we have stated, speed is a huge challenge to the crisis response and being able to quickly put a plan in place will put the business in a proactive position. Remember that a crisis requires action to be taken and the business must be seen to be actively dealing with what has happened. This action must also be clearly outlined in the crisis communication narrative. There is no place for a passive approach when responding to a crisis and hoping to deal with it effectively.

In Chapter 1 we went through what to include in a crisis communication strategy and how to approach it and ensure it is linked to the operational response plan. Put some time aside to ensure that you know the organization's approach to business continuity and crisis management. Having the right plan is something that can't be developed in isolation. Use the support in this book to develop a crisis communication strategy. But remember that it doesn't stop with this being developed; you have to share it across the business so that people know what it means and how it will be implemented. Plans are only as good as the people who will put them in place and their understanding of the response. Training and support as well as communication about the plan are all essential to embed it within the business. As organizations are dynamic and people come and go all the time it is a training and education plan that will need to be in place throughout the year and at key points in the lifetime of an employee, for example when they start, when they get promoted, etc.

Developing simple checklists that people can pick up at short notice to guide them in what they need to do can save valuable time. Create them as part of, or alongside, your plan. Keep them as stand-alone information sheets that can be handed out to whoever has to perform the role that is outlined in the sheet. The key is to have a plan and supporting documentation that can be picked up and used by communicators and non-communicators alike the moment a crisis occurs. It should also be simple enough for communicators from outside the organization to understand and act upon, as they may be brought in to support as additional resources. Remember to consider the use of language within the crisis communication to ensure it is clear and accessible as well as being inclusive and sensitive to those affected by what has happened. The plan and associated documents will come together as your crisis communication strategy and approach.

Prepare

Writing the plan isn't the end of the crisis response approach. A plan on its own is a theoretical analysis of what the business considers will be effective communication in managing the crisis. But that is just half of the story. Plans must be scrutinized, analysed, assessed and above all tested. It is the testing through exercises and crisis simulations that will turn a theoretical plan into a practical document ensuring confidence in readiness. If you have a plan, make sure you create the framework to pull it apart and rebuild it stronger and better for the moment it has to be used.

Training people to use the plan is the second phase of preparing the approach to crisis management. Anyone involved must have been provided with training through the testing and exercising process or as a stand-alone training session. If possible, make it part of job descriptions and continuous professional development for people across the business, particularly if they are in a management position and are likely to be leading sections of the crisis response. You can also provide training by asking those who have had first-hand experience of managing a crisis to come into the organization and share their learning and insights. Real-life experiences can provide a focus for what to review or develop, or how to stress-test a plan. Consider bringing in a crisis management expert from outside the business to help with this training element. Crisis management and crisis communication consultants can bring expertise and experience that will be able to stress-test the plan and the people who will lead it. They can provide bespoke training and support to assist the business in its development. This is important because the aim is to have a plan that is ready to be used and can provide a solid response but can also be added to in a crisis.

A key role within the crisis response is that of the CEO or leader within the business, who is likely to be the person who will be used for media interviews and who will be fundamental to the communication to employees. They may not do interviews at the start of the crisis but at some point they will have to be accountable to people as the head of the organization. The CEO and the senior management team may feel that they are ready and do not need any assistance but we can all benefit from additional training and support. So use your influencing skills to encourage them to be part of crisis response training, and crisis communication training specifically. It is always beneficial to have a number of senior managers or leaders within the business who have been media trained and are ready to deal with the pressures of media interviews during a crisis. Often leaders will appear to have seen and done a lot but, as we know, a crisis will be a one-off that many will never have faced or experienced. Leaders being seen to accept training will send a positive message to the rest of the business, who will also need to factor time into developing and preparing for a crisis. After all, leaders are role models to employees and have a responsibility to ensure the business is in a state of readiness to manage a crisis from top to bottom.

Process

Putting the right structure in place is important and goes beyond the roles and responsibilities that are outlined in the crisis communication plan. Chapter 3 considered the way those organizations who carry a lot of risk and face regular crises manage and communicate about them. Remember the structure does not have to mirror the usual business processes that operate within the organization, as this is a time of exceptional circumstances. Provided people know the plan and how it works then the structure can be implemented just for the crisis management and recovery phase. Success will come from having a structure that works for the way the business operates but that can be implemented swiftly in response to the emerging crisis.

The process must be developed ahead of any crisis occurring. It requires a clear approach to managing risk operating within the organization. Know the risks that exist and the ones the business may face and ensure these are kept regularly updated. It is everyone's responsibility to identify risks and make senior staff aware of them. The risk management process is your precursor to any crisis management work, as without it you cannot look at scenarios and develop appropriate and relevant testing. Investing time in the risk assessment and risk management processes can help to identify a crisis in its early stages and to mitigate the impact of it. This same risk management process can also prevent a crisis occurring as mitigation is put in place at an early stage limiting the impact of the issue and ensuring the business can get a grip of the situation.

It may feel like developing the process is not the responsibility of communication staff, and you would be right. Communicators cannot make this happen on their own, but they can play a key role as a catalyst to get the business in a state of readiness to deal with any form of crisis. They can ask the challenging questions, they can point the leadership to the actions being undertaken by others and they can highlight the impact to businesses that get it wrong. For additional support, learn from others and bring people in who can assist in developing the approach across the business. However, developing the risk management processes within communication itself is the responsibility of the communication lead. The professional communicator should be able to spot the signs of a potential crisis or critical incident and to share their concerns with the business so that mitigation can be put in place. Ensure you have an effective risk management system in place within your communication team.

Purpose

An honest and authentic approach to crisis communication means remembering the purpose and values of the business. The purpose is what the business is established to do, to deliver or to make. If you try to be something you are not when dealing with a crisis, it will be found out very quickly and will have a detrimental impact on perceptions of your response. Remember, authenticity is key, whether that is for the individuals leading the response, the CEO and the company spokesperson or the organization itself. Never try to create a picture of the organization that is not accurate and does not withstand scrutiny. Build the organization's purpose and philosophy into how you deliver the other four Ps of crisis communication.

Make sure you know what the situations mean to the people, plan and process that you are putting in place. Also, keep an open mind about how the purpose and philosophy of the business may need to develop and adapt, particularly when considering the response to a crisis and the feedback that was received. Learning from the recovery and the reviews of the crisis is important, and the business should be open to conducting some self-analysis when concluding a crisis.

The five Ps are all important to the totality of the communication including external, internal and stakeholder communication. External communication includes all forms of media, social media and direct communication as well as community liaison. Internal communication must always be at the forefront of considerations when a crisis emerges, particularly working with the employees leading on wellbeing and welfare support. But you must also remember to include stakeholders within the crisis communication plan so that they learn about what is happening first-hand from the business. They can also support you and create a mutually beneficial relationship. Of course, a strong working relationship with stakeholders should exist before any crisis happens and should continue long after the recovery has concluded. If you have a good operation in place to deliver communication as a business element of the organization this will assist greatly when you are under pressure dealing with a crisis. These elements such as stakeholder engagement mapping, channel strategies and even content strategies mean the crisis communication response has foundations it can utilize.

Maintaining readiness

Putting it simply, there should be an organizational priority that looks at the readiness to deal with a critical incident or a crisis. Operational plans for the business should mention the importance of being match fit and ready to face any critical issue or crisis to ensure the appropriate planning and training takes place. Making crisis response part of the organization's DNA and its business processes is the only way to be sure you are in a position to manage whatever the future brings. If you already have this in place, then great news – you are on the road to effective crisis communication. But if you don't then you need to make it happen.

Start by making sure the senior leaders and CEO are aware of the benefits of effective crisis communication and that they understand the risks from being ill-prepared. Case studies can assist in explaining what has happened in other organizations and where things have been beneficial or harmful to a business. The two elements go together. Show the positives of preparing for a crisis as well as opening their eyes to what could happen if things go wrong. In the case studies featured in this book you can see both the financial and reputational damage that can come from the crisis response. Done well, it can ensure there is a future for the business, but if it is done badly then it can mean a drop in share prices or a reduction in sales.

Remember to focus the discussion about crisis communication and the crisis response on what matters to the business, whether that is the bottom-line financial situation, shareholders' views or customer satisfaction rates. If you know what the organization values and how it measures operational success, whether it is finances, reputation or customer satisfaction, then you can frame the conversation to ensure you highlight the benefits of effective crisis communication.

Bottom up

If you are concerned about where to start, work from the basics and build upwards. If you are new to crisis communication, then you cannot expect to achieve everything overnight. Start by putting some basics in place, such as writing a crisis communication plan, and then be clear on the milestones that are required to build upon this as you progress. This is the roadmap that was mentioned earlier. Everyone must start somewhere in developing the crisis communication strategy and approach for the business.

Whenever a crisis occurs within another organization or business, take the time to review the communication that is put in place. Look at what that organization does and says. Consider how it deals with queries through social media. Review what information is provided on the company website and how this may change or be approached in different ways in different countries. Assess the media interviews undertaken by the CEO. Look at how quickly they were done, and what was said within the interview. Consider the narrative that is given on social media, to the media and provided in any other formats. All this can help you to recognize good practice and when a company may be slow or ineffective in the response.

Never be afraid to seek help. Few communicators will have direct experience of managing a crisis and getting support can allow you to tap into the learning and experiences of others. There are many crisis communications conferences and workshops around the world that can help provide an insight into how many situations have been approached. There are also specialist crisis communication consultants who can support the development of plans and any exercising and training, as well as assisting in considering the road to recovery. You may also want to speak to other organizations that you work with to look at their plans and see how they may support your work to develop crisis communication plans.

But remember that with all this learning and experience you can access there is no simple equation for effective crisis communication. You have to look at the specifics of the situation, the details of the organization and its purpose, and the communication that takes place day to day. All those elements will have an influence on how you approach and deliver crisis communication. You must have a bespoke plan in place: your plan and a plan for the business you are supporting. Put that time in your diary to start to consider and review the current situation and identify the work that needs to be done. Find the gaps and then find ways to fill them.

Do it now

Finally, there are five key things that you need to go and do now before you forget the details of this book and continue with your day-to-day work demands:

1 Ensure you know the organization's plans for dealing with a crisis and what your crisis communication plan looks like. Check they are up to date.

2 Take the key learning points and top tips within the book and look at them within existing plans so that you can see what may need to change.

3 Assess the risks that you may face and ask to see the risk management plans for the business, including any testing and exercise regimes.

4 Consider what training you may need to put in place or what support you may need to make things happen.

5 Prepare now and don't ignore crisis communication because you never know when a crisis will be upon you.

Conclusion

Developing a crisis communication plan that is ready to implement the moment something happens can feel overwhelming. Take some time to think things through and to ensure you understand the existing systems and processes. If there are existing crisis communication plans then consider whether they are up to date and would be ready to use. Do they mention the affected people? If they are not built around the people that will be affected, both public and staff, then they need to be immediately overhauled. Break down the thinking into five areas: people, plan, process, preparation and the purpose of the business. But above all keep the affected people in your mind as you are revising and rewriting the plans.

Create a roadmap that will allow you to take the steps to move forward towards developing an effective crisis communication strategy. Revise the existing plans or rewrite from your understanding of crisis communication and the business. Know what the milestones are that you need to reach to put the new or revised plan into place and be ready to act. Consider also how you will keep things up to date. This roadmap can become part of the annual business planning process and the communication objectives for the year.

Once the new plan is in place then the hard work begins of educating, training and exercising it. Involve employees in the crisis communication plan development and in the testing of it so that they can understand what it means for them and how they can support it. It is more likely they will remember what to do when a crisis emerges if they have had practical experience of what it means to them. The more scenario testing and exercising you can do the more likely they are to be ready to act. Education and communication about the plan are good but real experience in an exercise is much better. Leaders and managers must see the role they have to play in the crisis communication response. But don't neglect the education of frontline staff in what will happen because they are the interface with the public. Remember the importance of giving staff a list of customer checkpoints, where those are and the roles that are responsible for managing them. This will be invaluable when you need to respond quickly and alert them so that they can give an accurate and informed response to the public.

Finally, take the lessons, guidance and advice from this book and look at what you can take forward to implement. But don't let the learning end there; keep learning from what happens. Look at crises when they emerge and assess the communication response that is put in place. Identify what the priority is for the organization as outlined in its response. Consider who is the spokesperson – how do they look, what do they say and does it build confidence in both the response and the organization? Above all, remember you are not alone in trying to be ready to manage a crisis; there is expert help and advice available. Consider who may be able to help you from within the sector where you are working, from those who appear to have an effective crisis communication approach and from people who have communicated through a crisis. Remember to call on help from others as required as you move along the roadmap to implement an effective crisis communication strategy.

INDEX

The index is filed in alphabetical, word-by-word order. Acronyms are filed as presented; numbers are filed as spelt out.

CPSIA information can be obtained
at www.ICGtesting.com
Printed in the USA
JSHW041623270623
43861JS00013B/527

9 781398 609419